The Lower Limbs in Jungian Psychology

In *The Lower Limbs in Jungian Psychology: The Girl with Her Big Toe in Her Mouth*, Inácio Cunha explores the motif of lower limbs by amplifying their symbolism from a wide range of source materials, including an intriguing statuette from prehistoric Brazilian culture.

Taking a Jungian perspective, Cunha gathers and compares rich material from different historical, anthropological and mythological viewpoints, as well as from fetish, dreams, fairy tales and physical symptoms. Noticing how often the subject of legs and feet manifested in his analytical practice, not only as symptoms but also as dreams and fantasies, Cunha set out to deeply scrutinize our symbolic understanding of these body segments.

By observing the lower limbs in the context of evolution and their occurrence in mythology, he proposes a parallel between the evolution in the manner of walking in different species and the development of consciousness. Cunha also surveys dreams relating to these body parts in multiple manifestations, as part of complexes, fantasies and fetishes, and through the description of physical marks, spots and injuries. Mythological icons, such as Ulysses, Achilles, Oedipus, Jacob and others, are utilized to amplify the meaning of the feet and legs as far as their psychological meaning is concerned.

The book also explores the lower limbs as a sign of creativity and projection of creative power, before moving to investigate a clay icon from a pre-Columbian indigenous tribe, the Tapajó: an ancient statuette of a girl with her left big toe in her mouth. Cunha analyzes the relevance of this image as an archetypal pattern, occurring not only in his clinical work—in clients' dreams and physical and emotional issues related to their lower limbs—but also in other cultures' depictions of analagous representations in stories and images. The utilization of material gathered in his extensive research from multiple sources characterizes the method of amplification, advocated in analytical psychology as a possibility to extract symbolic meaning of a given image.

The Lower Limbs in Jungian Psychology: The Girl with Her Big Toe in Her Mouth is an original overview of a rarely examined part of analytical psychology and symbolism, and will have great appeal to Jungian analysts, analytical psychologists and psychotherapists interested in somatic, psychosomatic and symbolical understanding. It will also be of interest to academics and students of Jungian studies, psychotherapy, mythology, anthropology, history and symbolism.

Inácio Cunha, PhD, is a Jungian analyst based in Belo Horizonte, Brazil. He trained in Switzerland and the USA.

The Lower Limbs in Jungian Psychology

The Girl with Her Big Toe in Her Mouth

Inácio Cunha

Routledge
Taylor & Francis Group

LONDON AND NEW YORK

First published 2019
by Routledge
2 Park Square, Milton Park, Abingdon, Oxon OX14 4RN

and by Routledge
52 Vanderbilt Avenue, New York, NY 10017

Routledge is an imprint of the Taylor & Francis Group, an informa business

© 2019 Inácio Cunha

British Library Cataloguing-in-Publication Data
A catalogue record for this book is available from the British Library

Library of Congress Cataloging-in-Publication Data
Names: Cunha, Inácio, 1962- author.
Title: The lower limbs in Jungian psychology : the girl with her big toe in her mouth / Inácio Cunha.
Description: Abingdon, Oxon ; New York, NY : Routledge, 2019.
Identifiers: LCCN 2018044578 (print) | LCCN 2018046726 (ebook) | ISBN 9780429465826 (Master eBook) | ISBN 9780429879791 (Adobe Reader) | ISBN 9780429879784 (ePub) | ISBN 9780429879777 (Mobipocket) | ISBN 9781138610347 (hardback) | ISBN 9781138610354 (pbk.)
Subjects: LCSH: Consciousness. | Leg—Psychophysiology. | Leg—Symbolic aspects. | Mind and body | Jungian psychology.
Classification: LCC BF311 (ebook) | LCC BF311 .C865 2019 (print) | DDC 150.19/54—dc23
LC record available at https://lccn.loc.gov/2018044578

ISBN: 978-1-138-61034-7 (hbk)
ISBN: 978-1-138-61035-4 (pbk)
ISBN: 978-0-429-46582-6 (ebk)

Typeset in Times New Roman
by Swales & Willis Ltd, Exeter, Devon, UK

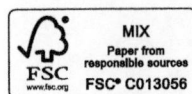

MIX
Paper from
responsible sources
FSC
www.fsc.org   FSC® C013056

Printed and bound in Great Britain by
TJ International Ltd, Padstow, Cornwall

This book is dedicated to Isabel, who knows the power of the feet, be they white, very white, or just big, really big.

Contents

Foreword

The liminal world of soul's body

The world we know, experience, suffer, create, lose, is driven by invisible forces which become available to consciousness only when we survey their effects, or they inhabit image and render it numinous. Just as the human ego splits the phenomenal and amoral world into opposites—declaring them good or bad—so we split body from soul, and live in the fractures which follow. In the hands of a skilled interpreter who sees through both biological and psychological lenses, we may recover a primal vision of the world as one. Dr. Inácio Cunha is uniquely qualified as a mediator of these worlds, and a guide to their healing.

The task of depth psychology is to track the movement of the invisible world through the forms of the visible. (This was once the task of the theologian as well.) Dr. Cunha's work is bold and imaginative, and very informative. How many of us reflect, for example, on what "bewitchment" might mean to a modern sensibility? Have we not dispensed with such superstition? But he lifts the veil and shows how any of us in the grip of delimiting complex suffers a form of possession, a state of bewitchment. Or how may we see the task of that energy system personified as "the hero" in each of us, that developmental impulse to overthrow the regressive urge of the unconscious, shake up the status quo, and move us forward in service to nature's intent.

How we learned to "stand up," "move forward," "walk on our own two feet," and so on are both wonders of bodily articulation and metaphors for our developmental and intentional agendas. The richness of human evolution is somatic, societal, psychological, and spiritual, and this book reminds us of the essential unity of all being.

One of the rich practices of Jungian psychology is the technique of amplification, which means to broaden and expand the resonance of any concept, image, movement, into its more comprehensive and deeper dimensions. Accordingly, we learn that the concept of "sin" derives from having taken "the wrong step," or it can mean "wounded feet," which was also the etymology of Oedipus as well. Through a rich summation of mythological accounts, we learn the role of feet and legs—their strength, their standpoints, their wounds—and thereby get a deeper sense of the power of this primal instrument we carry with us and learn to use in halting steps. We recall, too, that more words come from the Indo-Germanic root *sta*—found in *stand, substantiate, substance, understand,* and so on into the tens of thousands—than any other root concept. From the familiar cast of characters—Adam and Eve, Odysseus, Oedipus, Jacob, and myriad other non-Western figures—we remember our archetypal grounding in humankind's steps forth on this perilous earth. And our many halting, lamed steps as well.

Focusing on an indigenous statue unearthed in the Amazon basin, Dr. Cunha illustrates beautifully how the process of amplifying images restores that rich resonance of the archetypal field, even as we live an era of transient structures and values, seductive distractions, and numbing onslaughts. This statue of a girl with her toe in her mouth—homey, humorous, wistful, what? And how does the shaping of a sullen stone yet carry a scintillating aspect of the human spirit? Dr. Cunha's amplification of this image finds its parallels in many far-flung cultures.

In working once with the drawing of a schizophrenic patient who depicted himself as a sun-eating dragon, I found dozens of parallels in Eastern and Western imagery, suggesting again the archetypal field of energy, the timeless zone on which the spheres of both the personal unconscious and the thin wafer of consciousness so uneasily ride. Just as my patient believed this act of autophagous consumption would destroy an older, disabling world, and generate a new world with greater amplitude, so an amplification of this statuette points to the continuing energies of death/rebirth, regeneration, a Heraclitean passing, and a Heraclitean arriving.

Jung pointed out that symbols are the precious tools we employ to express what cannot be expressed, much less understood. Symbols allow us to approach the mystery of ontology, the paradoxes of being, and stand in relationship to them, even as they retain their sovereign autonomy. As Dr. Cunha points out, what nature asks of us is often appalling to the ego, but nature will be served with or without our cooperation. Discerning the mystery coursing beneath the surface of quotidian life restores depth to our journey, wonder to our ways, and a continuing summons to humble acknowledgement of our role in a large, and sacred, drama.

Dr. Cunha is a most able guide, and teacher, not only of the technique of amplification in depth, but of how the ordinary is in fact extraordinary. This exotic, curious girl with her big toe in her mouth proves to be our familiar, our semblable, our sister.

James Hollis, PhD
Washington, D.C.

Acknowledgments

Every time we start a new task, we confront challenges and obstacles at the same time. Then, we visualize and find the routes suitable to continue the ordeal as if they were a natural compensation for the initial despair. Writing this book is an example of such an endeavor. At the end, however, everything that was revealed in its course was appreciated as "the things" that had to happen. Otherwise, it would not have been the work that needed to be accomplished. Therefore, I would like to acknowledge the people and circumstances that, in one way or another, became seminal parts of this journey.

First, I want to thank the late Lucy Penna, clinical Jungian-oriented psychologist, who first introduced me to the richness of the Brazilian pre-Columbian art and the clients who generously shared their dreams and allowed me to mention them here in this book. Next, I would like to thank the participants and the lecturers who joined the Colloquium on the North-Brazilian Pre-historic Art, organized in Belo Horizonte, in 2007, to discuss the northern Brazilian pre-Columbian cultures. I also want to express my appreciation to the Emilio Goeldi Museum administration, in Belém, Brazil, for allowing me to visit the special collection section of this institution where the original Tapajoara statuette has been housed. I am also grateful for the support and encouragement that I received from the faculty of the Research and Training Centre for Depth Psychology According to C.G. Jung and Marie-Louise von Franz, in Switzerland, where I was trained as a Jungian analyst. I also want to relay my appreciation for the assistance and kindness of Susannah Frearson, who is a commissioner at Routledge in the area of analytical psychology. She made the task of publishing this book much lighter than I had anticipated. Last but not least, I would like to express my gratitude to Jennifer Phelps, who preciously and patiently helped me with my "Portuguesenglish" style of writing.

I also want to say thanks to the illustrator of this book, Flávio Carvalho Markiewicz.

Introduction

"How beautiful on the mountains are the feet of those who bring good news . . ."
(Isaiah 52:7)

The following text is the result of two converging conditions which fostered the investigation of the motif "lower limbs" under the light of Jungian psychology.

The first condition refers to the frequent and insistent occurrence, in the analytical setting, of subjective and objective questions related to the image of "feet" or lower limbs in general. There is a plethora of oneiric images referring to these bodily segments in their multiple representations, be they under manifestations as complexes, fantasies, or fetishes. More pragmatically speaking, there is also a tremendous amount of reports related to marks, spots, signs, or lesions in these limbs which ratifies the need to investigate symbolically such structures in a broader sense.

The dream reported below exemplifies part of this question. It is an oneiric image reported by a middle-aged man (45 years old) from his childhood. Even though he could not recall how old he was at the time of the dream, he believed he was about five, since he still slept in his crib:

> I was near what seemed to be a fountain or a pool of naturally warm water. It might have been inside a cave or in the interior of a mountain. I saw a man swimming in this pool, and he appeared to be a very important person (he looked like Elvis Presley). He sat on the edge of the pool, and then I could see his feet. They were very white, maybe slightly pink. Extremely beautiful feet! Beside him, I could see many jewels, gold coins, or something like that. I felt ashamed for thinking his feet were so beautiful.

He mentioned a feeling of ambiguity when he awoke, as he wanted to share the dream with his mother but feared she would not notice the numinous character of his experience. There was something prohibitive in this fascination that, later on, he equalized to a wound regarding his integrity as a man. Even though he didn't understand the dream, he somehow knew that its meaning was very important to him, and kept it to himself. He knew that it would be impossible to share this image with others, despite the emotional impact it caused, because he feared they would not understand.

Consequently, the image of the foot in this context, involving fascination, pleasure, complete lack of understanding, and terror, became a constant in this man's life. It was such a discomfort that he eventually sought analysis. The motifs of "feet" or lower limbs in general have constantly returned to his thoughts and dreams, or have made themselves present in his daily life through injuries in those areas (the patient has twisted his ankle several times, has had minor muscle fiber disruption in the calf, and has felt non-specific pain in his knees). Therefore, the recurrence of these images and events assured that, in principle, it was imperative that the accommodation and understanding of such symbols should not be postponed.

The second determinant condition that led to the investigation of this theme relates to a replica of a statuette which belongs to the Tapajó, a Brazilian indigenous tribe. This pre-Columbian object bears a peculiar register of the lower limbs. It represents a feminine anthropomorphic figure, holding her left foot against her mouth with both hands, as if she were sucking her big toe. The original image was found in the region of Santarém (a city by the shore of the Tapajós River, in the state of Pará, in the northern part of Brazil). Now it is under the custody of the Emilio Goeldi Museum. A replica was given to me by my wife approximately four years before I began my initial research on this subject.

This replica remained on my shelf, together with some additional reproductions of small funerary vases and other icons from the regions of Marajó and Amapá (an Amazon area also in the northern part of Brazil), for all this time until its presence became more imposing. The icon started to be discussed in a more systematic way after an additional dream related to feet was reported by another analysand. It was at this moment that a new possibility was created to discuss and to investigate more deeply the theme of lower limbs in relation to their psychological associations.

The more we pondered the image, the more hypotheses emerged. Could it be possible to propose a parallel between this bodily segment domain—keeping in mind its symptoms and its symbolic, oneiric, and literary representations—with the process of consciousness development? Could we comprehend the lower limbs above and beyond the act of locomotion? What does the unconscious want to convey when it utilizes so many images of these limbs in dreams or when it causes injuries to them?

After a preliminary investigation, a varied and frequent utilization of the motif of feet (including toes, calves, knees, thighs, and hips) and other forms of locomotion were found with a strong symbolic appeal in many genres of literature. In addition, several fairy tales, myths, legends, and sagas emerged, which contain representations of images and allegories of these parts of the body and point to conditions that extrapolate their primary function related to displacement. That is, these stories made use of the lower limbs to talk about power, deeds, suffering, and heroic destiny, for example.

The information regarding this Tapajoara statuette is, so far, rather precarious, primarily because it was found casually, and also because there are no formal or substantial scientific reports about it. It must also be emphasized that the study of the statuette occurred, initially, as a secondary interest. It was an epiphenomenon, which was triggered by the symbolical investigation of lower limbs during an analytical session. This icon became part of the scene in a synchronistic fashion. Somehow it constellated or, in other words, it added the energy that fostered the need to have a deeper psychological understanding of these bodily structures.

The investigation of this statuette should also be understood as a way to honor the artistic production of the pre-historic Brazilian culture. The attempt to understand such material allows it to become more vivid in our present lives, and helps us to have a broader comprehension of our own identity. Such material was produced previously to the European colonization and it is still germane to, if not the very translation of, parts of our souls. Even today, very little is known about the autochthon peoples from the Amazon basin and neighboring areas. Any time a nation or a culture establishes connections to its primary sources, a more robust identity is built up. The material that has been so far gathered from Marajó Island, Tapajós River, Maracá, and many other primordial cultures in Brazil should be taken, therefore, as a possibility for a more solid historical, geographical, temporal, and psychic centering that appears to be so feeble in this tremendously extroverted and globalized, modern lifestyle we embrace nowadays.

In the first chapter of this book, the lower limbs are discussed from a phylogenetic perspective and their evolutionary development is analyzed based on ontogenetic implications. Keeping the different forms of locomotion in mind, the abandonment of the waters as a metaphor is utilized as a process parallel to the acquisition and development of consciousness.

In Chapter 2, the lower limbs are discussed through a mythological lens and different cosmogonic myths that make use of these bodily segments are emulated in their symbolic aspects. The occurrence of lesions or marks on these limbs are also presented in order to corroborate the hypothesis that these bodily regions house the projections related to psychic progression or stagnation, as well as the creative or transforming destiny of those who bear a heroic personality.

The third chapter is primarily concerned with a more specific condition related to unipedalism (or monopedalism), and brings to the forefront the symbolic idea that such a form of bodily sustentation or displacement suggests a higher level of consciousness.

Chapter 4 discusses the Tapajoara statuette, beginning with its objective aspects, such as its physical structure, plasticity, and artistic content. Additionally, in order for more knowledge of this icon to be gained, some anthropological, historical, and theoretical material is presented.

Based on the material gathered and presented in the previous chapters and their pertinent associations, Chapter 5 investigates this Tapajoara icon through the lens of further symbolic understandings.

Chapter 6 focuses on the importance of the universe of the foot and its symbolic representation in the Tapajoara image. In addition, the creative quality of having the foot in the mouth is emphasized.

The last chapter presents the final considerations of the study.

It must be highlighted that the central objective of this study is to try to extract psychological meaning from oneiric and iconographic images that bear strong symbolic appeal. The practice of Jungian analytical psychology presupposes the assemblage of material from different but convergent domains in order to subsidize the attempt to understand a given content from the psychic point of view. This is what characterizes the method of amplification proposed by Jung. It allows that analog contents, originated from different cultures or regions of the planet, can be interpolated while trying to extract a symbolical sense of a given image. The amplification becomes, in some senses, a study of compared anatomy, which also makes use of bodily structures from an already known species in the attempt to understand a given structure of a new species that has not yet been known.

Chapter 1

The lower limbs in the context of evolution

From a phylogenetic point of view, we can say that the appearance of limbs in the Phylum Chordata is the result of the gradual change from a liquid ecosystem to a solid one. The movement beyond the waters was accompanied by a progressive sophistication of the central nervous system, which allowed the living being to dwell in a number of different ecosystems. It required the development of distinct features, in accordance with the characteristics of each environment. The proliferation of new species, their migration, and continued development of their skills were possible and successful as long as each of them was capable of moving to and from other ecosystems.

In the waters, motion is feasible merely by the use of fins or body twists, since water's resistance is rather low. But once locomotion presupposed a solid environment, living beings developed bodily appendages that could "articulate" the need to travel on a surface with more intense attrition compared to the waters. Were it not for these articulations, it would be very difficult or even impossible for some species to move around on the surface of the Earth. In this way, the limbs can be seen as structures that allowed a continuous act of conquering the land, and a progressive abandonment of the waters at the same time.

From a psychic point of view, waters can be understood through myriad forms. In this context, the water itself, and all that is in it, is one of the most pervasive symbols among all others that refer to the unconscious, be it individual or collective. Waters have shown themselves to be a never-ending source of life, while also being a place where everything else can be accommodated. This element is a primary representation of the processes of life generation, death, and regeneration.

From a biological point of view, the animals that do not return to the water for reproduction developed procreative systems and structures that are capable of containing water, such as amniotic fluid or the white in an egg. Our survival also depends on water and there is no substitute for its lack. Hence, it would be fascinating to discover what powers in the evolutionary process made the aquatic species leave the waters in favor of the land. What could have overcome the natural state of inertia of the marine beings and compelled them to abandon such a vast and generous ecosystem in favor of dry and firm soil?

It is therefore no surprise that various cosmogonic myths have a lake, a river, or an ocean in the background. Quite often, when the gods became extremely annoyed with their children, they would send terrible waters to destroy them and to eventually regenerate the whole creation. Thus, water is itself a place with no differentiation where everything can happen, everything mingles in, and everything is confused. Using this line of thought, it is symbolically significant to say that learning to deal with the waters or leaving them means acquiring some degree of differentiation; that is, consciousness.

It is also important to note, however, that the unconscious, like the waters, tends to encompass everything. In order to separate from the primordial matrix, or the Great Mother, a fight of mythological proportions must occur. Psychologically speaking, She who creates all also wants to keep all to Herself. In the unconscious, the opposites are both nourished equally; the creative act of the unconscious has the same energetic power as the act of destruction. It is up to the individual to make use of his/her faculties in the attempt to keep this inner opposition well-balanced, thus avoiding self-destruction.

Through her interpretations of fairy tales, Marie-Louise von Franz shows us the avaricious and dubious aspect of the unconscious. She says that some bewitched beings (an allegory for the obliteration of consciousness and situations where we are tied down by complexes) may regain their human form (conquest of consciousness) when redeemed; nevertheless, the process may be sometimes incomplete or hampered. While returning to his or her former appearance during the transformation process, the individual may still retain a wing, scales, or a tail, and often loses a limb or other body part. This is, from a psychical point of view, a reference to the power of retention, frequently contrary to progress, which can be also observed in the unconscious.

Parts of this process can also be seen in schizophrenia. In this condition one can observe a tremendous creativity that is made recognizable by the richness of the images available to the individual. In turn, it can reveal a situation of intolerable psychic and moral suffering due to the destructive aspect of such impressions. A person suffering from schizophrenia may even make attempts to end his or her life or act against others. The main feature of this pathological condition is an almost complete loss of the capacity to judge; since the ego structure is too feeble to hold the tension, the psychic processes have their autonomy enhanced. The patient becomes overwhelmed and is overcome by the contents of the unconscious.

Hence, a heroic disposition is required to deal with the devastating power the unconscious may reveal. The presence of the image of the hero is, in itself, an affirmation of the plurality of the unconscious. If, on one hand, the unconscious is regressive or contrary to development, it also offers a progressive figure of the hero, which is a model of functioning for the ego, whose aim is to change the "status quo" of one's psychical life. The hero brings remediation for the condition of inertia, marasmus, or psychic malfunctioning.

Returning to the evolutionary discourse, one can see a gradual, though not universal, liberation of the upper limbs in relation to the lower ones, as far as the walking function and the role of supporting the weight of the body are concerned. The quadrupeds, especially those on the lower scale of neural evolution, typically use all four feet for locomotion. In the mammalian class, principally, it is possible to find the upper limbs being used to manipulate objects, besides helping with locomotion in conjunction with the lower limbs. This situation reaches the highest point in humans for we no longer use our hands for locomotion; the feet are our major means for transportation.

Ontogenetically speaking though, because of the absence of claws human feet have lost their predatory character. They became more susceptible to bruises and cuts or had decreased celerity on rough land due to lack of a suitable horny coating. Human feet are also more sensitive to changes in temperature due to the absence of scales, fur, or feathers. Mobility in treetops is jeopardized by a decrease in skill and prehensile ability of the toes, greatly appreciated in other primates. Therefore, human feet may be classified, under the evolutionary view, as one of those segments that did not incorporate the advantages present in other species, which were important to their survival.

On the other hand, by not incorporating those abilities, humans had the ability to stand up and walk on two feet, thus relieving the weight from the upper limbs. So, in spite of losing strength and robustness, this adaptation allowed humans to be deft with their hands, distinguishing them among other mammals. These adaptations gave human beings the chance to more effectively and efficiently process the gains in their neural system.

In this way, we can use the means of locomotion, which enabled living beings to separate from the waters towards the land, as a parallel metaphor for neural development and the acquisition of consciousness. In other words, the less bounded to the waters and the more the lower limbs are used exclusively for locomotion, the more neurologically developed that living being may be.

This evolutionary line of thought, which up to now has focused on the locomotor function of the limbs, can also be appreciated from a psychic perspective through a mythical tale that deeply influenced the Freudian psychoanalytic movement. This is the story of Oedipus, utilized by Freud on its romantic aspect. Using the allegory of locomotion, only a passage from the myth (the riddle posed by the Sphinx) will be analyzed in relation to psychic development. In the myth, the monster (the Sphinx) posed the following question to Oedipus: "Which animal walks on four feet in the morning, on two feet at midday, and on three feet in the evening?" Oedipus answered: "Man: as an infant, he crawls on all fours; as an adult, he walks on two legs and; in old age, he uses a 'walking' stick."

The role of the Sphinx in this tale is dubious, as she can either kill or let someone live (the lack of differentiation akin to the unconscious). Lack of knowledge or providing the wrong answer would result in death. But life and redemption would prevail by just uttering the word "man," since the quiz refers to the way a human being moves about from childhood until older age.

When we consider the way that the Sphinx proposes the conundrum, we can see that she actually pronounces an evolutive declaration. It is as if she is saying: "Look here, you may have your life spared only if you understand that it is man who, as he moves along the path of evolution, is the agent of his own redemption!" What the Sphinx conveys is that an infantile human being (both biologically and psychically) is too close to the ground, and is nothing more than an animal-like creature, a quadruped. The Sphinx teaches Oedipus that a human being must stand up and disidentify from the gods (without being completely bound to the ground), in order to reveal his human condition.

On two feet, then, man's gravitational center shifts upwards, and from this position he can walk upon the Earth. He must endure a long journey, live intensively, and expand his consciousness. In this process, he may build up and strengthen his identity and, eventually, he may even reign among other species. In this posture, he experiences, one might say, an ego apotheosis. But, somehow, such a place may also lead him to some degree of self-waning. Quite often, a man will trample on his own self-assumed grandeur, for eventually having thought of himself as a deity. Here then is where the sense of losing ground comes back again.

As life goes by, the assertive ego starts to fade away and man finds himself somehow weakened and not fully able to accommodate the immense scope the soul imposes on him. His gravity center has now moved a little ahead, and he is forced to bend over, for his point of support escapes him. He seeks to keep his balance, which is now outside ego consciousness, possibly, closer to the encompassing center of psychic activities of the Self or a God Image. However, he approaches this Center with a certain caution, here represented by the stick, that is, an extension of his own conscience, or even a widened consciousness. He then walks on a three-point base of support. The stick would function as a tool to allow one to get closer to that Center without succumbing to the all-pervading unconscious until it is the moment when one fatally is caught by it, for death meets the human being in a region where consciousness has no governance! Thus, aging and bending over may convey, in this context, the acquisition of a superior form of consciousness, no longer centered in the ego. It is the time for the gods, now seen from a different angle, to deal with the demands of the soul!

For both the Hellenic man of the fifth century BCE and for the Christian, standing up to the gods presumes evolution. For the former, it is evident from the Oedipal myth that this man requires the stick to avoid losing himself within the totality of the gods. This stick could be understood here as an instrument or means to make possible the relationship between the individual and the powers which are perceived inexorably outside the previous apotheosized ego. In Christian tradition, however, man must return to a state of extreme inner pureness; he must become a child again, so he may meet the gods once more. The Hellenic god has not yet been transformed; he is full of paradoxes, hence the lack of complete submission on the part of the man who still keeps his stick, as the Sphinx pointed out. The Christian god, nevertheless, is one-sided; evil is left out, and man can return to the welcoming god with no reserve, bearing a purified heart. As the Gospel of Mark states, "Whosoever shall not receive the kingdom of God as a little child, he shall not enter therein" (Mark 10:15).[1] But even here, one can see the idea of progressive evolution. Human beings must reach adulthood first, and then return to childhood.

Therefore, in an allegorical form, it is possible to propose an association between the process of acquisition of the lower limbs (their differentiation, level of neurological sophistication, and varied ways of locomotion observed across a

Neuromotor   Consciousness   Supra
Development   Acquisition   Consciousness
                                           (unio mentalis)

Leaving the waters

Quadrupedalism ⟶ Bipedalism ⟶ Monopedalism

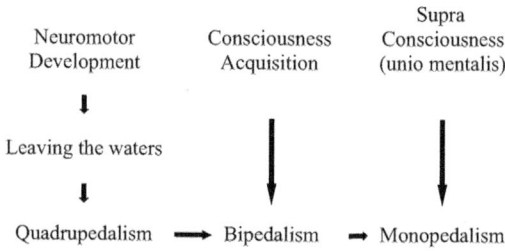

Figure 1.1 Locomotion and the acquisition of consciousness.

variety of living beings) and the blooming of consciousness as seen among human bipeds. On the other hand, mythical and religious literature still offers images of unipedal beings, which allude to an ulterior state of consciousness. Obviously, we do not find such beings in nature that would biologically correspond to this conception. Usually, their actual representation is made possible by some artifice such as accident, disease, imagination, and so forth. But once this representation exists, it supports the projection of an excelling consciousness which presupposes something that transcends the objective world upon which we tread. In the alchemical tradition, for example, the state of *unio mentalis*, that is, a higher level of psychic development, is represented by the monocoli, or uniped beings.

In the following chapters, biological evolution will be looked at symbolically in an attempt to demonstrate that the change from a two-limb to a single-limb locomotion may suggest an important development in human consciousness. Figure 1.1 summarizes the parallel between locomotion and the acquisition of consciousness.

Note

1 Mark chapter 10 KJV (King James Version). (n.d.). Retrieved March 02, 2018, from www.kingjamesbibleonline.org/Mark-Chapter-10/. (From now on, the author, chapter and verses will be stated within the body of the text.)

Chapter 2

The occurrence of lower limbs in mythology

In Chapter 1, we explored the Sphinx's riddle in the Oedipus myth as an allegory of the evolutionary process, based on the manner of walking. In this chapter, we will examine additional stories that use the image of the lower limbs in a different context in order to illustrate their symbolic connections with distinct processes related to psychic development. If it is possible to observe both the legs and the feet as appendages which enabled individuals to move around and eventually free themselves from the original matrix, then it is not without reason that they are the preferable locus to be wounded. Usually the vengeance for the separation between matrix and progeny, or the unconscious and ego consciousness, is directed at the legs and feet. Thus, it is not difficult to recognize why so many myths make use of some kind of molestation, wound, or deformation in that region of the body in order to register this severance.

In the mythological universe, a lower limb injury can be, simply put, either the result of one's fight to separate from the generative forces, or a token to keep alive the memory that refers to the attempt by such forces to prevent the breakdown. Thus, lower limbs can be considered the preferential bodily segments that need to be sacrificed in the process of becoming conscious.

The lower limbs and cosmogony

The following paragraphs show various situations where the lower limb is the tool for creating this world or, from the psychic point of view, is used for acquiring consciousness with its due consequences.

According to Aztec mythology, before humanity came into existence, the world was covered by water. Tezcatlipoca and Quetzalcoatl lived in the heavens, and Tlaltecuhtli, the Great Caiman, lived in the deep waters. Tezcatlipoca, who was a Trickster, one day decided to make Tlaltecuhtli come up to the surface. He dipped his foot into the water to attract the monster's attention. Suddenly, Tlaltecuhtli caught the foot in her mouth, and held Tezcatlipoca fast. Then a fierce battle broke between them. Tezcatlipoca lost his foot while Tlaltecuhtli's jaw was irreversibly fractured (Figure 2.1).

Figure 2.1 Tezcatlipoca (drawing based on the Codex Fejervary Mayer, National Museums Liverpool).

Because she was injured, she could no longer submerge in deep waters, and thus land, as we know it today, was created. The human race spread in the folds of the caiman's skin, which eventually became the hills and valleys that cover the earth.[1]

This myth emphasizes certain aspects that are important in understanding the foot motif from a psychic standpoint. First, the myth makes use of the feet as the creative motor of the universe that humans inhabit. In other words, the feet have the necessary creative force or the initial "kick" to begin humanity. Second, it indicates that creation presumes a fierce battle with the primordial monster. And third, it becomes clear that the separation/creation of the world indicates a sacrificial condition in which the newly created world is always in need of further amelioration. This myth also conveys psychological and symbolical messages. Psychologically speaking, a new image is engendered out of the clash between the opposing forces within the unconscious. Symbolically speaking, when that which is above meets that which is below, each one of these two things loses something to the other, so that a third and completely different condition is created.

The so-called creating god, Tezcatlipoca, loses his foot and substitutes an obsidian mirror for it, which is his allegory (he is also known as the Smoking

Mirror). With such a mirror, his condition of omnipresence is affirmed. Therefore, in spite of the sacrifice of his foot in order to create the world, Tezcatlipoca reveals the imperfections of creation and establishes the need for a continuous acquisition of knowledge. It must be noted, however, that the newly created world is still imperfect and further creations will require continuous and renewed heroic acts. Replacing Tezcatlipoca's foot with a mirror implies that humanity will forever need a partnership in the heavens, which reveals that the search for one's own being must be done in a reflective manner.

In this way, the feet symbolically represent a person's point of view or how one stands in the world. Injury or loss of the feet can be understood, therefore, as a scratch on someone's world view, or as a need to adjust oneself to a new world that is opening up to the individual. After any damage to the feet, an individual has to modify his or her habitual way of treading in order to consider the new road that has opened up. Hence, when Tezcatlipoca offers his foot to the Great Caiman, he not only facilitates the creation of a new world, but also brings into existence a new way of perceiving it. The lesion or loss of his foot becomes the sign of this separating process.

Laurete Séjourné sees the loss of Tezcatlipoca's foot as part of his destiny as a creator. Since he personifies the nightly or earthly Sun, every time this god comes to earth he mutilates his foot as if some part of this star were losing a part of himself. Therefore, "the missing foot synthesizes the infinity of divine particles scattered among humanity; and the misty mirror would be the symbol for the reflection of a hidden reality," that is, a reality that still needs to be worked on.[2]

This Aztec myth has a collective and universal value, and reveals images that belong to a deeper level within the unconscious processes. It is as if the myth were talking about the very beginning of creation, for the main actors of the drama are mythical and animalic figures. Human beings are only mentioned, as group, towards the end of the narrative. There is no individual, per se. Therefore, this myth illustrates an act of primordial creation—the dawning of humans' consciousness.

In a different cosmogonic myth found among the Araweté, another Brazilian indigenous group, it was said that Tadide, the wife of Aranãmî, threw away the footsteps of her husband that were on the stones.[3] Feeling insulted, he decided to leave the place where, up to then, mankind and gods lived together. He took his rattle and started dancing and smoking, and the earth began to rise. That was how the celestial vault was created and humans were separated from the divine beings. It is not clear why Tadide acted like that, but symbolically speaking it meant that the standpoint of the god was no longer fulfilling. Humankind needed to differentiate from the divine.

In the great cosmogonic Judeo-Christian myth, some situations similar to the Aztec myth can be observed. Creation occurs on a more advanced level since human beings (Adam and Eve) are already present, yet not totally differentiated in relation to the creator. Therefore, the kind of consciousness to be created should warrant the individuality of the human condition, distinct from the divine, but paradoxically forever entwined with it.

The mythical being that brings about separation between the human and the divine is the serpent. Soon after the psychic integration of the fruit from the Tree of Knowledge, Adam and Eve acquire consciousness of themselves. For inducing this act of separation, the serpent is severely punished in its manner of locomotion:

> And the Lord God said unto the Serpent, 'Because thou hast done this; thou art cursed above all cattle, and above every beast of the field; upon thy belly shalt thou go, and dust shalt thou eat all the days of thy life.'
>
> (Gen. 3:14)

From this passage, one can assume that the serpent had feet beforehand, but with the punishment, it had to start sliding along the ground (Figure 2.2).

Both human beings and the serpent are punished for their sins, but the serpent has to suffer the more regressive blow. It is worth mentioning that the word meaning "sin" in Portuguese is *pecado*, which is derived from the Latin *peccō*. Etymologically, *peccō* means "to give a wrong step" or "twisted foot," which signifies a difficulty in walking. It can also be observed that, upon bringing about consciousness to mankind, the snake is condemned to move about on the ground and, as part of the hostility established between itself and human beings, a human's ankle would be bitten by the snake (Gen. 3:15). In a tautological way, humankind and the serpent both have a punishing mark of separation: humans on their feet (or ankles) and the serpent in its lack of feet. Again, a new world (new consciousness) is created as inexorably imperfect.

There are several ways in which we can examine the imperfections of the Judeo-Christian world, which are outside this discussion. However, I will mention that after leaving the perfect Eden, the "imperfect world" the human beings are now aware of is a world in which the process of becoming conscious is in its very early stages and calls for a progressive improvement. The separation from the divine implies that we need to come to terms with our flaws and engage in an ongoing process of polishing.

The so-called "hostility" between humankind and the serpent can also be analyzed psychologically. According to a Gnostic myth, it is believed that after being expelled from Paradise for having tasted the fruit from the Tree of Knowledge, human beings will eventually return to Eden to eat from the Tree of Life and then become like God. The Gnostic allegories show the serpent as a prefiguration of Christ. (This can also be seen in the Bible, when Moses was told to build a pole and hang a Brazen Serpent to sort out the ones who would be saved—Nm. 21:8–9.) Therefore, the fact that the snake is always "searching" for a human's foot to bite might be understood as the longing for reunion of that part of ourselves from which we have been separated. This includes the instincts from which we have become progressively alienated, which causes all sorts of neurotic behavior nowadays. Perhaps we shall only return to Paradise after being whole again— when the human and snake parts of ourselves reunite. Therefore, the poison of the snake may be understood here in an antinomic way, as an *elixir vitae*, for it must

Figure 2.2 Paradise (drawing based on the painting by Hugo van der Goes, 1440–1482, Kunst Historisches Museum Vienna).

kill (that is, transform) every mundane and collective aspect that we acquire while living on earth, which actually saves us from our sins, as Christ himself eventually did. To return to Paradise means that we must be whole again, and this will only happen when the Christ/Serpent mends what has been separated.

The injury to the lower limb as opposition to progress

In the above-mentioned myths, the injury on a lower limb stands out as a token for the effort put into cosmic creation. But any attempt to injure or to cripple the lower limbs can also be understood as anti-progress, or as an effort to abort separation. It is as if the unconscious wants to punish any separation trial. Jung, in a seminar on dream interpretation, declared that images of wounds or injuries on the legs suggest that the individual's evolution process has been hindered.[4]

In the Danish fairy tale "The Princess with the Twelve Pair of Golden Shoes," the stagnation in the developmental process is made evident by a lesion on the lower limb. The story is about a young man who travels through the world in search for adventure, until he comes to a town where the walls are covered with skulls of men who had been sentenced to death. He learns that the princess of the kingdom went out every night and returned in the morning, having worn out twelve pairs of golden shoes. But no one in the kingdom knew how or why.

The young man went up to the king and offered to find out what the princess did every night. The king told him that if he could discover where the princess went and what she did, then the young man would receive half the kingdom and marry the princess. The young man had to stay in the princess's room and remain awake, but had no more than three nights to complete this task. To test his alertness, the young man's heel would be pricked with a golden needle, and if he was asleep he would not find out the secret and would be sentenced to death (like the previous suitors whose heads lined the town's walls). The first two nights, the young man fell asleep despite his best efforts, but on the third night he stayed awake, pretending to sleep and resisted the prick of the golden needle. He then followed the princess through three kingdoms, and finally saved her from the possession of a giant. In the end, the princess is rescued, the giant is slaughtered, and the young man becomes king.

This fairy tale brings up a set of images and ideas that are characteristic of the unconscious and sketches out the background from which the conscious manifestations are brought about. We can infer from the narrative that the prevalent conscious condition in this tale is characterized by an imprisoned and unredeemed feminine function, who, consequently, becomes rather destructive. She not only avoids marriage, but also kills each one of the candidates. The masculine principle is de-potentiated (a lesion of the heel); its consciousness is obliterated (deep sleep) and is on its way to perish (death of the suitors). It is known from the famous story of Achilles that the heel is an especially sensitive area "behind the individual, so he cannot easily see that part of himself (it is where one is unconscious of oneself), and . . . the heel is part of the foot, which is associated to his point of view."[5] Therefore, the wound on the heel symbolically represents the culminating point of obliteration of consciousness on the part of the suitors, which in this case means death or, metaphorically speaking, being retained in the unconscious. However, the hero in the story stays awake (does not lose consciousness) and manages to prevent the story from ending in complete obliteration of the masculine principle, that is, death (decapitation). He saves himself, frees the princess from the power of the bad giant, and becomes king.

Another story that illustrates how a foot injury hampers the dynamic flow of life is that of Philoctetes, the figure of the eminent archer. He was one of the Argonauts on his way to the war of Troy (Figure 2.3).

However, he was deserted by Agamemnon and his companions on the isle of Lemnos because of the intolerable smell that exuded from a wound on his foot. There are different versions as to how this wound came about. One of them says that Philoctetes had become the depositary of Hercules's bow and arrows after his death because he had lit the funerary pyre and kept the secret of where the hero's ashes were hidden. Hera, taking revenge for the honors given to the bastard son of Zeus, sent a serpent to bite his foot. Another version says that he was bitten by a serpent while walking carelessly over the sacred ground of the nymph named Chryse (or Lemnos), for he was the only one among the travelers who paid no honor to her, and also refused the love she offered him. And a third version states that after he revealed where Hercules's ashes could be found, he injured himself with one of the hero's arrows (poisoned with the blood of the Hydra), which fell from the quiver onto his foot. It is said that Philoctetes remained alone on the island for ten years until Ulysses discovered that only the weapons that had belonged to Hercules, now in the possession of Philoctetes, could help win the war of Troy. Hence, Ulysses and his men returned to Lemnos and convinced Philoctetes to join their group again.

In "The Princess with the Twelve Pair of Golden Shoes," the suitors were killed for not making good use of their consciousness, that is, they fell asleep. With this attitude, these individuals lost the opportunity to discover what the princess did to wear out her twelve pair of shoes and were then swallowed up by the unconscious. The feminine principle, in the quality of the anima (the princess), who was in a possessed state, was not "handled" in a thoughtful manner. While the candidates that were sent to rescue the princess succumb to sleeping, the model of the masculine principle's functioning is morally questionable; the suitors do not make the due effort to fulfill their task. In the myth of Philoctetes, the masculine principle is also incapacitated by the powers of the unconscious, either by the Great Mother (Hera and the sacred ground), or the anima (Chryse). However, in Philoctetes we can see a model of a rather inflated ego, with a certain degree of arrogance regarding the contents that are greater than it. It is even possible to say that a religious attitude is missing in Philoctetes. Jung uses this myth to explain how rejecting the unconscious can bring drastic consequences for the individual: "Its instinctive powers, when continuously ignored, become

Figure 2.3 Philoctetes (drawing based on the painting by Jean Germain Rovais, 1763–1788, Musée des Beaux-arts).

powers of opposition . . . to evolution."[6] For instance, Chryse/Hera turns into a poisonous snake, or Philoctetes poisons himself with Hercules's arrow which falls on his foot. Then the punishment begins. In the fairy tale, the weakened masculine principle ratifies the possession of the anima (the princess) by a sterile and destructive masculine principle (the giant). Therefore, when masculine consciousness does not relate properly with the anima, she associates in the unconscious realm with a rather hypertrophied, obtuse, and destructive animus.

In the myth, Philoctetes was bitten by a snake when he walked carelessly over the sacred ground of Chryse. The need to be respectful towards the sacred ground can also be observed in the biblical myth of Moses (Ex. 3:1–6) where he was advised to take off his sandals when he approached the spot where the bramble bush was aflame. Psychologically, the removal of the shoes suggests that there are times, in the presence of the divine, that we must abdicate the ego's standpoint. Taking off the shoes can be likened to freeing ourselves of any kind of mask, especially the one by which we "carry over" our feet, that is, our stand point.

There is yet another motif to be explored in the Philoctetes myth: the nasty smell that exudes from his wounded foot. In Chapter 1, the feet were equaled to appendages, which could be considered noble as they allowed humans to stand upright and use their hands freely. However, as human feet grew more fragile in comparison to the feet of other animals, human beings had to artificially protect them by wearing shoes. The human foot then became an ideal place for the growth of microorganisms, rendering a disagreeable smell. And so, in Jungian terminology, the price to be paid for bipedalism, or its shadow, is the unpleasant smell. (Of course, other painful biomechanical consequences related to the erect position also emerged, which mostly affect the spine.)

The unpleasant odor coming from Philoctetes's wounded foot has an important symbolic value since the olfaction among living beings provides a vital function. In searching for food, detecting the presence of predators, or the capacity of discovering the fertile period of the female for procreation, living beings use smells in their everyday survival. Thus, for the male, the olfactory function is necessary for coupling and guaranteeing the continuation of the species. The odor, identified as something pleasant by each member within a given species, is one of the most important erotic connections between each member. Odors may also indicate weakness, and there is a great probability of sick or old animals being abandoned or chased away as they can no longer add to the survival of the group due to loss of energy, or because their scent enhances the risk of attack by predators, putting the whole group at risk. These animals can be "discovered" in the midst of the group due to a specific odor that they discharge, which relates to their impaired condition.

This datum may be corroborated by the fact that dogs have been utilized to detect ailments in humans (especially certain kinds of cancer).[7] Because of their non-familiar odor, animals of rival clans are generally detected and eventually chased away. Through smell, an individual may belong to a group, or not; there is procreation, or not; or an animal may build up its identity in relation to its rival group, or inside the hierarchical organization of its own group.

In this way, odors are the great messengers of Eros. But from a phylogenetic point of view the olfactory function in humans is quite primitive. Its representation in the cerebral cortex is rather small and its differentiating capacity is weaker than hearing or seeing, for example. Nevertheless, even though this function is not well developed in humankind, there is an important investment in the industry of perfumes as a way to compensate for such a deficiency.

Metaphorically speaking, the modest sense of smell in humans can be associated with a less differentiated perception of psychic phenomena, that is, those that are closer to the unconscious. Dreams that portray lesions in the nose or the inability to detect odors could be related to a hindering of the function of consciousness that is related to intuition. These types of dreams speak to an important disconnection from the instincts. When something has been intuited, we might say, "This smells like this or that," or if we feel that something is not quite right, we may say, "This does not smell good!" We might even say that a person has a "good nose for business."

Another aspect to be taken into consideration regarding the motif of bad smells is the confusion they can create. Among the remaining population of the Maya culture in the Guatemala highlands, there is the tale of a supernatural being called Mam or Maximon, who, among other features, spreads out a nauseating smell in all directions so as to establish confusion, ambiguity, and disorder. Among several physical deformities, this creature has crippled legs and is lame. It is also said that Mam's feet are turned backwards due to his exaggerated and perverted sexual behavior (homosexual practice).[8] Thus, in Philoctetes, we have the wounded foot as an allegory for a standstill in the evolutionary process of the hero's life story, and an intolerable smell, which indicates an injury to the erotic capacity of the man who is disconnected from the creative matrix or the feminine.

In the Bible, we can also find other stories that allude to the integrity of the feet (or the lack thereof) in association with a halt or continuity in the flow of life. The prophet Daniel, when interpreting King Nebuchadnezzar's dream of a statue with feet of half-iron and half-clay, reveals the varying aspects of the kingdom to the king:

> The feet and toes Your Majesty saw, partly of iron and partly of clay, mean a divided kingdom. It is as hard as iron, for Your Majesty saw iron mixed with a part of clay. The toes, half of iron and half of clay, mean a firm kingdom on one side, but weak on the other.
>
> (Daniel 31:41)

Psychologically speaking, this meaningful image represents a reconciliation of opposites. It shows that Nebuchadnezzar was indeed able to bring together the opposing forces of strength and weakness. In a way, his point of view stands on the awareness that the opposites are a reality to be faced, although they require integration. And by integration, it presupposes that the characteristics belonging to each isolated aspect are able to impregnate each other so that a *tertium no datur*, or the reconciling "third," can emerge.

The mark on the lower limbs as an indicator of a transforming destiny

So far, the lesion of the lower limbs has been discussed as an indicator for the splitting process, creation, and jeopardizing the development of mythical beings or individuals involved in each specific drama. In the general literature today, we can find several examples of heroic personages whose destinies are revealed or marked by a physical sign or lesion, especially in the lower limbs. The next section looks at how these lesions or marks on the lower limbs exist in order to identify or stamp one's fate to engage in the continuous process of psychic development. As observed with the cosmogonic myths, the newly created world is rather imperfect and it is the hero's job to continue the creative process or transform the already established reality.

Ulysses

Ulysses is one of the most well-known representatives of the mythical world who bears a scar on his thigh as a mark of his fate. *The Odyssey* states that he got the scar after being attacked by a wild boar during a hunting season with his paternal grandfather, Autolycus. Ulysses also knew about the prophecy of the oracle that said he would go on a long journey and take a long time to return home. So, when Menelaus called his men up to rescue Helen of Troy, Ulysses pretended he was insane to avoid his fate, but all in vain. He had to fulfill his destiny and joined the fleet. Later, when he returned to Ithaca to reassume his land and his wife, he disguised himself as a beggar. He was recognized by his nurse while she washed his feet because she was the one who had cared for him years before, treating his wound when he was a child.

The drama of Ulysses is so vast and dense that another study would be necessary to render proper justice to the fullness of the symbolical meaning of this mythical figure. But for now, what matters is the fact that he had his heroic destiny stamped by a mark on his lower limb. In psychological language, what can be seen in *The Odyssey* is the perennial struggle for deliverance that human beings had to endure against the protean aspects of the unconscious. Jung says that what is completely unknown in men is the unconscious, which can also be seen as the feminine. Therefore, it is part of humankind's endeavor to discover an equidistant point where we can properly relate to the unconscious. This point should be distant enough to protect us from being swallowed by it, but close enough to avoid being petrified in our existence, since the unconscious is also the never-ending source of life.

This laborious encounter with the unconscious/feminine can be observed in different scenarios in *The Odyssey*. Ulysses, while still young, was attacked by a wild boar, an animal that is frequently associated with the feminine. Swine, in general, are often present in the worship ceremonies for the Great Goddesses in different cultures. In the Greek pantheon, for example, Artemis, Demeter, and

Atalanta are portrayed with a sow by their side. In Celtic mythology, the goddess Brigid is associated with this mammal for it encompasses both the fertility and aggressive nature that is inherent to this beast. In Hindu mythology, there is the javelin-faced goddess Varahi, who protects the gates of the Nepalese temples. With Ulysses, we can see the varied forms the "feminine" takes in someone's life, through the different women he related to. There was, for example, the accommodating aspect as seen with his wet-nurse who took care of him as a child. Then, Helen of Troy, whom he eventually had to redeem; and Circe and Calypso, with whom he had to be entangled in order to acquire self-knowledge. He was recognized by the feminine as the man of Ithaca (his wet-nurse again), and lastly, he had to reunite with the feminine (both as Penelope, his wife, and as Ithaca, his homeland) in order to fulfill his destiny.

With each of these women, Ulysses had to go through a great number of challenges, or different learning processes under the feminine's breviary, before he could rest. He was both a partner and an opponent of the unconscious personified in the feminine until he reached psychic maturity and established a *coniunctio* with Penelope. Symbolically, this means that he could finally relish a life under the auspice of the Self. The heroic deeds of Ulysses's life are very meaningful for Western man's psyche since these tasks encompass the redemption of the masculine through the rescue of the feminine in his own soul.

The kernel of his drama can be traced back in the *imbroglio* at the Garden of the Hesperides, during the banquet, where the feminine acts in a rather pernicious way. Eris, the Goddess of Discord, was not invited to the party, meaning that only the pleasant aspects of the feminine were allowed there. This, however, is seen as a violation to the feminine principle who wants to be taken as a totality. If the dark side of any principle cannot be included in someone's life, this aspect will sooner or later fight back. So, Eris offers a golden apple to the "most beautiful" among the other goddesses present, and then the problem begins. Zeus, foreseeing the dangerous outcomes of judging such a contest, deferred it to a human being. Paris, with his naïvety and short reflexive capacity, chooses Aphrodite, the goddess of love.

At this point, some aspects should be highlighted: one is related to the fact that this contest required human consciousness to be solved; second, the kind of available consciousness was not developed enough to keep an adequate distancing from the problem, so it became entangled in an archetypal problem. One of the greatest problems with poorly developed consciousness is that it either identifies with the archetype (taking up the role of Zeus) or is too naïve, so that it is overcome by the gods. Had Paris been conscious enough, he would have avoided such a role!

When Paris elects Aphrodite, he reveals how far his psyche is able to reach, which seems to be no further than instinctual satisfaction. By choosing the most sexualized aspect of love, a psychologically immature man excludes all other nuances available in a relationship between the masculine and feminine principles. This goes far beyond an affair between man and woman. As a rule, though, any psychic content that is excluded by consciousness will return, sooner or later, claiming back its share in this realm. Paris then becomes the victim of both his identification with Zeus and his actual choice, and is possessed by the lascivious aspect of love, which is quite damaging. He breaks down the matrimonial alliance at Menelaus's house, steals Helen, and brings destruction upon his own people. The amount of damage caused to the Eros principle by Paris's attitude can only be evaluated by the proportion of destruction seen with the Trojan War. A man is not always aware of how much the feminine principle can get hurt and become deeply revengeful and lethal whenever it feels neglected or dishonored. In man's psychology, the feminine is commonly perceived as "exaggerated" in its reaction. But empirically speaking, this is the actual dimension the feminine assigns and it reacts to the negligence suffered.

Thus, Ulyssess' role in the epic is to remedy the damage to the one-sided and unreflected attitude that Paris demonstrated. From a psychological point of view, Ulysses is that aspect in us that has to give up the comfortable and predictable existence in favor of a necessary maturation, so that the opposites can be reunited in the collective consciousness. In men, he represents that aspect which, while rescuing Helen, visits the most improbable recesses of human life until he is psychically mature enough to deserve Penelope's love. From a Jungian perspective, a man must come to terms with both the anima and the real woman. Simply put, this identifies a man who is able to bring forth the best of his creative wealth by being able to acknowledge, to relate, to learn, to bear, and to love the other's totality that makes him whole. This is individuation!

Achilles

Another mythical figure who was predestined in his lower limbs is Achilles. Thetis, known as the "Goddess of the Silver Feet," was prophesized to bear a child whose heroic deeds would exceed his father's. However, instead of bearing a child from a god, she was forced to conceive from a virtuous mortal. After Achilles was born, she would not accept him as mortal, so she dipped him in the River Styx, holding him by the heel (Figure 2.4).

Achilles grew up with a body that was invulnerable, except for his heel, which later was the cause of his death.

It had also been prophesied that the war of Troy would only be won after a hero named Achilles died in it, quite young but full of glory. Thetis, aware of this, sent her nine-year-old son, dressed as a girl, to the palace of King Lycomedes to live among the king's daughters.

In general, mother-goddesses such as Thetis often attempt to halt their sons' emancipation, thus causing them some sort of debilitating psychic or physical wound. According to von Franz, the motif of wounding the son so that he will not leave and abandon the mother is a common feature in fairy tales and legends, and also in many real mother–son relationships. Often times, the wound that is inflicted by the mother, either through excessive care or neglect,

Figure 2.4 Thetis immerses Achilles in the Styx (drawing based on an engraving/etching, Johann Balthasar Probst, 17th to 18th century, Fine Arts Museums of San Francisco).

may lead to important psychic or physical compromise, whose hallmark is the de-potentialization of the son's masculinity. Sending Achilles to be raised as a damsel is one such example.

Even though Thetis bathed Achilles's mortal body in the caustic waters of the obscure river of the underworld, he still retained the reminiscence of mortality in his heel. The expression "Achilles heel" is rather common in many languages when one wants to characterize a situation in which a weak spot is present. Psychically, it means that the "untreated" part in Achilles (that which is overlooked in our psyche) reveals his (our) fragility. This is an issue of great symbolic value, for it shows us that "any condition obtained with some merit not coming from one's own efforts will necessarily have an intrinsic flaw."[9] Achilles is dressed and educated in the company of the princesses, daughters of King Lycomedes, and without his heroic destiny, he might have been known only for being Patroclus's lover.

The story of Achilles may be one of those which can be easily retrieved when the mythical question of feet is taken up. There are certain taboos among solar figures of heroes or gods, in which the feet are considered a place through which all the sacred essence of the figure can be lost. In other words, these figures are forbidden to touch the ground with their feet. According to Frazer, "The physical substance or fluid coating the sacred man can be lost when He touches a great conductor such as the earth."[10] And so, Montezuma in ancient Mexico, the traditional Emperor of Japan, and various tribal kings in African or Asian villages are all carried either on a litter or on the shoulders of their subordinates, so as not to touch their feet on the ground. This attitude was also kept by King Louis XV of France, known as the Sun King, who introduced the use of high-heeled shoes in order to keep his heels off the floor. Other figures, such as the Giant Antaeus, need to keep their feet touching the earth—the Great Mother Gaia—all the time in order to draw strength.

In Achilles's myth, it cannot be observed that the heroic imprint bears primarily the need for separation from the creating matrix, or that this matrix had turned against the hero in a vengeful manner for having been neglected or not suitably revered. More importantly, we can see a hero who is deeply loved by his creator, and her desperate actions to avoid his fleeing from her bosom. In this specific case, the mother-goddess wants to turn her son into an immortal creature so he may live forever with her in Olympus, and prevent him from going out into the world in search of adventure in order to meet his destiny (being killed prematurely in battle). However, it must be emphasized that a precocious and glorious death is also part of the script to be fulfilled by sons who are overly attached to their mothers. There is, indeed, a movement *beyond* the mother, but it is without a masculine fundament that imparts substantiality to the quest.

Achilles also bears characteristics of the offspring whose bond to their mothers reflects their relationship with the world. He behaves as someone who is always accustomed to having everything and everyone at hand at all times. Achilles had great difficulties with authority and was quite susceptible when his desires were not satisfied at once. For example, he showed unreasonable rage and insanity when he continuously dragged Hector's body around the castle after killing him, which demonstrates how merciless Achilles could be in relation to his enemies. Then, Priam had to beg Achilles for his son's dead body with great humiliation in order to provide a decent funeral.

In spite of Achilles's heroic destiny, his myth reveals an important psychic condition of not being able to redeem oneself. As previously mentioned, Achilles did not have to work for his immortality or earn it himself. Instead, it came as a gift from his mother and, psychologically, he was retained in her hands for it. He never matured as a man. His path was too emotional and poorly reflective. And this is what can be verified among many men who, in principle, are perceived as brilliant but cannot step outside the bosom of their mothers. They are often moody and carry on an unfulfilled life, incapable of building solid relationships or letting their creativity flow.

Oedipus

The Greek tragedy of Oedipus is another well-known mythic story that describes the Swollen Foot (from Greek *Oiden*, "to swell," and *pous*, "foot") survivor and his misfortunes. He is one of the solar heroes who also bears the pledge of the bondage to his mother on his feet. This story also recounts a prophecy: the son of the king who will grow up to kill his father and wed his mother. Fearing the prophecy, Oedipus's father commands that the child be killed at once. But instead, Oedipus is left to die by being hung upside down from a tree. Like any other hero, he survives and ultimately fulfills his destiny.

As a child, there was no indication of any intense feelings of love between Oedipus and his mother, as in the myth of Achilles. Oedipus was taken not because the Great Mother clearly wanted to protect him, or because the feminine had been overlooked. Instead, the maternal figure was quite contaminated by the prevalent masculine principle, which pervaded the conscious condition in the Hellenic world; that is, by Logos. Queen Jocasta gives in to the ideation of King Laius, and it is not clear whether she allowed her son to be taken to sacrifice for fear that he would someday kill her husband, or if she was terrified by the idea of becoming her son's wife.

However, in this myth we can see the same dynamic mentioned above, but problematized on a different level, as far as the mother/son bond is concerned. The motto here is the need to separate the forces more akin to the new consciousness (Oedipus) from the undifferentiated powers or the unconscious (Jocasta). The great difference compared to the above discussed refers to the fact that in this myth it is Oedipus who moves towards the unconscious instead of the unconscious pulling him towards itself in a boundless way. So far, the marked hero has to fight against the generating matrix, but it is also the hero himself who moves towards this matrix in order to fulfill his fate.

We can analyze Oedipus's destiny in two different ways. First, his tragic fate can be seen as the natural ending observed when the progeny is not successful in the process of separation from his mother. The notorious crippling of a man's masculinity is illustrated by succumbing and becoming the mother's "lover." Oedipus blinds himself as a self-punishment, and this blindness may be viewed as an equivalent for emasculation/castration, or as a variant for homosexuality and/or death. In myths where the narrative deals more with gods, that is, is more germane to the deepest processes of the unconscious, one can observe that the son-lover more often pays with his own life (or becomes literally castrated) for the price of this romance (Adonis and Aphrodite, Astarte and Tammuz, or Cybele and Attis). Under this view, Oedipus's tragedy can be understood as an aborted separation attempt between mother and son, with all its drastic consequences. It is aborted because, despite all the strategies Laius offers, he cannot evade the parricide, nor can Oedipus avoid the incestuous marriage.

This triangulated romance formed by Laius, Jocasta, and Oedipus constitutes the basis for Freudian psychoanalytic theory. In a simplified way, Freud postulated that the source of neuroses lies in the prohibitive dynamics of love and hate the son feels towards his mother and father respectively. The intensity of these feelings and the conflict they bring about, which culminates with the desire of union with the mother and death of the father, is either "solved" (repressed) and/or becomes pathologized due to the eventual prohibition of an outer realization (the incest taboo). In other words, the play of the powers leading to incest, with its inherent damaging consequences, or the eventual success in prohibiting it, all depend on how the "conflict between the instinctive demands and the forbidding reality" are dealt with.[11] The non-fulfillment of incest would be, therefore, at the service of cultural development. The first step towards creation of consciousness presupposes separation from the powers of the unconscious, not a union. Incest, in Freudian terms, would be, therefore, an allegorical regression in to the primordial matrix, the unconscious.

In this way, the tragedy in question would be a graphical representation of a psychic condition inherent to the not-yet-transformed and undifferentiated consciousness/unconsciousness which, therefore, reveals itself to be destructive. The story, due to its pamphletary appeal, justifies the timelessness of a theme that has been greatly reinforced by the Freudian theory of neurosis. The realization of incest in this story is not only the ratification of the opposition the unconscious exerts as far as progression/separation from it is concerned, but also the inertia or indolence of the new content which, paradoxically, longs to be forever attached to the generating matrix.

Incest and its gruesome implications were displayed over a thousand years previously in the cults of Astarte in ancient Phoenicia. Why does this theme, which caused so much appeal in the fifth century BCE, continue to be part of psychological and philosophical investigations after another 2,400 years? The answer may be that the essence of the contents played up in the myth has not yet been fully integrated into consciousness, that is, not fully understood. Thus, other forms of discussion on the subject are necessary.

As such, a second way to look at this drama is through the principles postulated by Jungian psychology. Analytical psychology provides tools that may contribute to a broader understanding of the Oedipus myth as it favors a less tragic or dramatic interpretation of the theme and views the subjects on a mostly teleological premise.

In this manner, the characters of the myth could be considered as functions of the psyche. Oedipus, Laius, and Jocasta might be seen as cohabitants or orchestrators of our lives, serving as psychic complexes whose effects are perceived on a personal level instead of the collective level. We might ask ourselves, "What are Jocasta, Laius, and Oedipus in my psychology, and what does each of them urge in me?"

Oedipus might be considered the psychic function which engenders the new, or something that is yet to be developed. This function strives to express itself and become conscious or realized. Laius, in turn, might represent the function responsible for establishing and maintaining certain attitudes that assure stability or at least a psychic identity in someone's psychic economy. In the myth, the function represented by Laius develops up to a certain point and then seems to be unable to sustain itself any longer. It acts as if it were wearing out, or failing to fulfill its purpose. Laius as a psychic function somehow cannot incorporate the newness brought about by an incipient consciousness announced by the Oedipus function.

These two functions are in opposition to each other; the Laius function strives to remain dominant on one side, while the Oedipus function fights to overcome its opponent on the other side. In an effort to keep up the status quo of psychic life, the Laius function fights back and appears as a threatening factor. It incorporates the tendency to cut off the novelty announced (the archetypal image of the castrating father is abundant in poetical and mythological literature—see Chronos, Saturn, Hamlet, King Minos, and so forth). Whenever an existential pattern loses its meaning and stiffens, and the flow of life halts, there is a call for the renewal of that pattern. The Laius function embodies the principle to be renewed while the Oedipus function embodies the renewer.

If the Laius function is more potent than the Oedipus function, it signifies the latter's demise (and Laius's actual objective in the tragedy). In this way, the Oedipus function would be nothing more than an intention. When the Laius function is murdered, however, it might be seen as the psychic equivalent of the individual's evolution towards the acquisition of new behaviors, attitudes, actions, and relationships, since the Oedipus function or newness prevails. Once the Oedipus function demonstrates that it is more vigorous than the Laius function, the newness "makes sense" for the psychic economy and, therefore, overcomes the function which is no longer tenable. The victory of Oedipus points to the process of psychic transformation.

It is necessary, though, to see in the Laius function, as with any other psychic structure, both a progressive and a regressive aspect.[12] In the previous paragraphs, it is only considered in its regressive aspect, that is, as an inner disposition which tends to prevent, castrate, and destroy. When the Laius function as the masculine principle tries to prevent the union between the Oedipus and Jocasta functions, we must ask ourselves a few questions: What is the intention implicit in the background of the psyche? Is there anything beyond just zeal enacted in this father/son conflict? What would be the final meaning of the Laius function in someone's psyche as far as its positive aspect is concerned? The answers to these questions might become clearer if we take a closer look at Jocasta.

Functionally, Jocasta represents the feminine in the psyche and, as such, it gestates the novelty once it receives the seeds of new ideas and nurtures them. Jocasta cherishes that which is to be born, makes it grow, and allows the newness to be disseminated. However, in its negative aspect, the Jocasta function is compared to the archetype of the devouring and terrible mother who suffocates, paralyzes, and eventually eats up her offspring. In its regressive state, this function represents the psyche in its shadowy chthonic aspect. The extreme accommodating aspect of the Jocasta function may have a nullifying effect on anything that approaches it, or may even lead to a complete absorption of what it bears. It may bring about retrocession and lameness to any incipient psychic development which has yet not attained enough strength. Without a disambiguating factor, this function could magnetize and annihilate everything. Erich Neumann uses the image of the serpent biting its own tail—the Uroborus—to represent this aspect of undifferentiation pertaining to the terrible mother.[13] The Laius function, then, can be seen as the first warning sign that the encounter with the Jocasta function can be dangerous and fatalistic. The fight between the Laius and the Oedipus functions has, then, an initiatory aspect, that is, it prepares the novice for the forthcoming challenge.

Another, more objective, approach to these functions is to think about all the new ideas or projects we promise ourselves from time to time. If such new ideas, projects, or tasks (the Oedipus function) are not abandoned precociously because of what is already ingrained and solidified in us (the dominance of the Laius function), they may eventually have a chance to become stronger and to flourish. However, these new ideas can also encounter great resistance or obstacles when they are just about to be concluded or when they are ripe enough to fructify. The germ of the new idea arises after fertilization, but it needs to be gestated (the Jocasta function). Sometimes, we might satisfy ourselves only by conceiving an idea. With great pleasure, we might rest upon a project, only fantasizing the "brilliantness" that will come out of it.

An example might be a person who has the most enlightened idea of writing a book, and even puts down a few lines (the Oedipus function overcoming the Laius function), but never manages to get past the first paragraph (the shadowy and devouring aspect of the Jocasta function). The ideas of this person belong only to the realm of possibilities—the terrible aspect of the Jocasta function— and are easily aborted in the presence of a fragile character or ego. However, when the Jocasta function is in its prospective aspect, it can be the most accommodating principle which welcomes the germ of new life. Then it is possible that the creativity announced by the Oedipus function does yield its fruit. Perceiving the Jocasta function in this way may be one of the greatest contributions offered by Jungian psychology, as it presents us with a chance to understand the return to the matrix, or the regressive motion towards the primary creative powers, as an important and significant act for the transformation processes.

But what about the Oedipus function? How can it be characterized under the domains of the progressive or regressive forces? Because the "Swollen Foot" is the novelty, the creative capacity—that thing recently created in the psychic universe—it heralds the transformation, and thus its progressive aspect. However, according to our discourse, the Oedipus function has not yet been sufficiently strengthened. It is only half-done! Although it escaped the castrating sword of the old ways of acting, it still seems to be weak or immature since it cannot endure the results of its actions. Oedipus is not strong enough to admit that to complete or build something up requires sacrifices and sacrificers. This Oedipus does not even "recognize" that in the background of the incest relationship is the idea of endogamy, the premise of which is to maintain the purity of the royal classes across the descendants, just as the gods avoid mixing with the "mortals." Thus, this particular union would ensure that the new arising ideas have an immaculate quality, and rebuff their corruption. Through the extensive analysis of myths and legends, Jung demonstrates that together with incest there is the inexorable urge for rebirth and transformation.[14] However, Oedipus "narrows down" his deeds to nothing but a murder and an illegitimate union. At this moment, he sees himself as both the one who gives in to indolence and to the comfort offered by the Jocasta function and as a parricide (insecure, and above all, guilty of having taken a step towards the future and of having been an instrument for the acquisition of a differentiated form of relationship with the world). This is when Oedipus blinds himself, an act that is commonly equivalent to self-castration (as previously mentioned), a form of self-imposed death, or living a sterile life.

It is worth saying, however, that there are other versions of the tale. In one of them, in spite of Oedipus being aware of his union with his mother, there is no subsequent complication to be observed, and nothing disagreeable happens to him.[15] He lives the life of a king, quite happily, until the end of his days. So, in this new version, it can be concluded that this Oedipus psychically "integrated" the death of his father and the union with his mother, thus engendering a prosperous nation. The absence of guilt in Oedipus for the death of Laius indicates that the Laius function needed to cease to exist. Or if it indeed needed to continue to exist, it must do so in a lower profile or a state of de-potentiation. In this other version of the myth, the marriage shows that Oedipus saw in Jocasta the most powerful and efficient symbol for the generating principle: the positive mother. What could be a more immediate, intense, and real experience of that which is nourishing, accommodating, and welcoming than the experience of a nurturing mother? If we look at these qualities on a personal level, it could be said that an individual who psychically defeats an aging order, that is, overcomes a moment of inertia (killing the Laius function) and weds that which is most fertile and nurturing (the Jocasta function), is a person who can fructify from a psychic point of view.

As we analyze mythical stories to better understand them, it is possible to observe that each myth deals with distinct strata within the depths of the unconscious. We can see this not only in the way the narrative is constructed, but also by the selection of personages. Every time we become more conscious of one of its contents, new facets constellate from different levels within the psychic fabric. Therefore, we can surmise that we are always supposed to be on a move towards life, that is, movement is an inexorable human condition as far as psychic development is concerned.

For example, when we compare the Aztec myth of Tezcatlipoca with Oedipus, we might be only digging about 100 meters deep with Oedipus, while we might be dealing with contents buried several kilometers below the surface with Tezcatlipoca. In Tezcatlipoca, the characters are all mythic and bear little or no resemblance to human beings; humans only come into existence after the creation of the world, and so the contents are well bedded into the depths of the collective unconscious. In the myth of Oedipus, there are human characters with social functions (king, queen, son, fatherhood, etc.), but also mythic figures, such as the Sphinx. In contrast, the characters in Tezcatlipoca developed their line of actions in a more direct manner with less morality from a human point of view; the two monsters do battle in order to create the world. In Oedipus's case, the main motif surrounds the prohibition of incest, a theme that is processed much closer to a conscience or morality that is under construction. If Tezcatlipoca's main issue is "to create consciousness," then Oedipus's issue is to build up morality within this very consciousness. By comparing these two myths, we might see how they both utilize the feet as symbols, and deal with the creation of consciousness at distinct levels.

Jacob

As we leave the Hellenic universe behind, it is also possible to observe the theme of a mark on the lower limb as an indication of a transforming future. In Judeo-Christian mythology, Jacob, for example, is born holding his brother's heel (in Hebraic, 'agev).

In Genesis, Esau, the firstborn of Rebecca and Isaac, is followed by his twin brother, who is then given the name Jacob (in Hebraic, Ya'aqov) (Figure 2.5). Esau, whose name refers back to the abundance of hair (in Hebraic, 'Esaw means "hairy"), was destined to live a country life and hunt, being his father's favorite. Jacob stayed under the tents and became the keeper of domestic animals, being his mother's favorite. With the help of Rebecca, his mother, Jacob obtained the right to have the grace of being the firstborn by tricking both Esau and Isaac. Interestingly enough, the Hebraic meaning of Ya'aqov is "that which supersedes or prevails." Afraid of his brother's wrath, Jacob fled to the house of his uncle on his mother's side and stayed there for many years until he was summoned to fulfill his destiny. It is necessary to say that he needed to remain under his uncle's service all those years until he matured into manhood. For a good part of his life, Jacob remained a "mummy's boy," but then he turned into a man and married.

After he became a real man, Jacob had to return home and meet his brother in order to confront his previous acts. But when he was halfway there, he found himself alone by the side of the Jabbok River, where:

Figure 2.5 'The Twins of Isaac', Maître François, c. 1475–80 (with permission by Den Haag, Museum Meermanno).

a man wrestled with Jacob until the break of day. And when he saw that he could not prevail against him, he touched the hollow of his thigh; and the hollow of Jacob's thigh was out of joint, as he wrestled with him. And he said 'Let me go, for the day is breaking.' And Jacob said 'I will not let you go, except if you bless me.' The man asked him 'What is your name?' And he said 'Jacob.' And he said 'Your name shall be called no more Jacob, but Israel: for as a prince, you have power with God and with men, and have prevailed.' And Jacob asked him, and said 'Tell me your name.' And he said 'Why is it that you ask my name?' And he blessed him there.

(Gen. 32:25–29)

For Jacob, the battle with the angel contains several aspects of initiation. At this moment, he has clearly reached a certain degree of maturity and is able to sustain a fight without the earlier tricks and help he had from his mother. It seems that Jacob has now integrated part of his mother complex. Not only is he wounded on the thigh, but he changes his name. The wounded area is quite significant, especially for the Hebrew people, since the thigh is a synecdoche for masculinity. It is the metaphorical organ of creativity, more so when related to a man. In other cultures, the thigh can also be considered an organ of creation. Zeus, for example, carried Dionysius to term by sewing the unborn child up in his own thigh; Hephaestus was born from the thigh of Hera; and the Nile River was originated from the thigh of Osiris. Thus, Jacob's thigh being out of its joint is equivalent to the circumcision of the penis, the most important mark among the Jewish people in their alliance with Jehovah. And, according to the classicist Richard Broxton Onians, the head of the ancient Greek people contained a "vital substance" (psyche), which could also be found in the thigh; in this way, sometimes the image of a skull with two long bones (femurs) crossed over it was treated as if it was the living remains of a dead person, only much later being used as a sign of death (pirate flags).[16] Other amplifications can be found among pre-Hispanic Mesoamericans, the Nahuas, who believed a vital force could be found in the back portion of the lower leg (the calf); the verb meaning "to devour a victim" meant literally "to eat the calf."[17]

The thigh has further symbolic value for Hebrews, especially when Abraham bids his servant to keep his hand under Abraham's thigh so as to seal his commitment to his master (Gen. 24:9). As an organ charged with Mana, the thigh can be further appreciated in the Apocalypse (Ap. 19:16) when it is said that the He who is the "King of the Kings and the Lord of the Lords" has these words written on His thighs. The figure of the redeemer, Christ himself, who will annihilate the evil forces in the last days, is also identified by a mark on his thigh. In Medieval Christian lore, the figure of the Grail King has a bleeding wound on his thigh. In essence, the wounded thigh sums up everything that is barren, dry, sterile, and gloomy, which claims his redemption. Here, the source of Mana, the thigh, is wounded and nothing else may come out of the infertile king.

Jacob's wound has a particularly special meaning, for it is not an open injury, and there is no blood. It is an inner lesion, a joint that has been disarticulated. Biomechanically, the hip joints have a primary function of attaching the upper part of the body to the lower part, allowing the individual to move about in an erect position. An injury to the hip indicates the need to change the body's center of gravity in order to maintain balance and locomotion. Symbolically, this means that the person is now called to change the way he had previously stood up and walked in life; that is, he is now invited to have a new and different perspective. A hip lesion implies a profound change in religious attitude in favor of psychic totality. With Jacob, it becomes evident that "he who was wounded is the chosen one."

Symbolically, Jacob can be seen as the part of the psychic economy where the progressive and transforming aspects of the unconscious insist on becoming known. However, the figure of Jacob could not be conceived without opposing powers—represented by his twin brother and his father (who preferred Esau)—and the difficulties he had to face, such as being in his uncle's household, crossing the river, and the fight with the angel. The doubling motif, when Jacob and his twin brother appear together, is a characteristic which reveals the urgency of content that wants to be "known." Jung says that whenever there is a doubling in dreams, something is emerging into consciousness, possibly in the imminence of becoming more clearly understood by the dreamer. Jacob exemplifies the regressive movement towards the generating matrix which reveals itself as nurturing, but also needs separation. The battle with the angel is a trial where he demonstrates the acquisition of a certain degree of maturity; therefore, Jacob appears as a transforming psychic function. Despite all the inertial forces that hinder his development, Jacob finds the necessary support in maternal love, assimilates it without perishing, and demonstrates that he is able to concretize his destiny. As far as the mark on the lower limb is concerned, Jacob's mark is more prospective than Oedipus's mark; Jacob succeeds, while Oedipus succumbs.

The marked lower limb as a sign of creativity

It is no wonder that the individual "chosen" by means of an injury on his lower limbs almost always has an extra dose of creativity so as to fulfill his destiny. Quite often, to overcome the forces contrary to progression, one needs to count on an unprecedented amount of creativity (Ulysses's guile to overcome all obstacles present in his journey; Jacob's wile in disguising his arm with lambskin to be blessed instead of Esau; Philoctetes's mastery of bow and arrow, etc.). However, this section does not necessarily refer to the kind of creativity that is required to solve urgent problems. Instead, creativity is referred to as a form of expressing psychic contents not yet revealed, bearing a collective impact. That is, the lesion on the lower limb is a mark of those who are the harbingers of the immense creative power of the unconscious; they are, in a certain sense, the revealer of the unconscious.

We see the lesion/creativity theme most frequently in the image of Hephaestus who, as mentioned earlier, was born from the thigh of Hera (Figure 2.6).

Figure 2.6 The crippled feet of Hephaestus (drawing based on a vase c. 550 BCE, Kunst Historisches Museum, Vienna).

When Zeus gave birth to Athena, Hera jealously decided to beget a child by herself, too. However, Hephaestus was born with deformed lower limbs (a club foot or lameness), which was a completely unacceptable condition for the standards of perfection set by the Olympian gods. In one version of the story, Hera throws the child in the sea with extreme rejection because he was considered the "last" of the gods and the ugliest as well. In this condition of rejection and agony, Hephaestus learned the art of metalwork and thus became the greatest artist among the gods. Despite his ugliness and physical impairment, he learned to work with fire and the forge, producing ornaments of rare beauty, until he was again "discovered" by his Olympian companions and was summoned to build them thrones of gold.

According to Edinger, Hephaestus is symbolically the aspect in our psychic economy that has to "keep its feet on the ground," that is, to be connected to reality, in order to flourish. The fall of this god from Olympus implies that his entelechy is meant to be actualized on a concrete level, rather than in the abstraction. On the other hand, Hephaestus represents "the creativity emerging from a deficiency or a necessity and so becomes especially precious to humankind, once he offers the imperfect man a partnership in the divine kingdom; a partnership related to creativity."[18]

Similarly, we have the story of Chiron, the centaur, born from the union between Chronos and Philyra. According to the legend, Philyra was a cousin to Chronos, who wooed her constantly. To avoid incest, she turned herself into a mare, but without success. Then, a creature was born—Chiron—half horse, half man, who was, consequently, rejected by his horrified mother. Chiron was then educated by other gods, acquiring knowledge in several areas, mainly in the art of healing.

As if this first ordeal was not enough, Chiron also spent his life trying to find relief for a pain in his foot caused by a lesion that Hercules inflicted accidentally with an arrow. In spite of spending his whole life seeking a way to remedy the suffering he endured, he found no relief for that pain, thus becoming the great mythic physician. Among Chiron's students was Asclepius, who became the patron of medicine.

Chiron, like Hephaestus, turns his wound into creative potential and embodies the idea that only the one who really suffers may be able to find a sound cure. However, in Chiron's tale, there is another important nuance to be observed. It was said that he could only obtain relief for his pain if he gave up his immortality, which he did by exchanging places with Prometheus, who was chained up in Mount Caucasus. As retaliation for stealing the divine fire and giving it to humankind, Prometheus was supposed to endure the eternal ordeal of having his liver devoured during the day and being regenerated at night. He could only escape this punishment if an immortal offered Prometheus his or her immortality, which Chiron did. Chiron's narrative symbolizes the transformation of individual pain into a quest for collective deliverance from suffering. Moreover, by offering his immortality to Prometheus, Chiron embodies the sacrificial figure *par excellence*, and in this context offers a new dimension of suffering that can only be relieved when it is brought down to a level closer to humanity. In other words, Chiron is one of the most important mythological figures that illustrates the value of deflation. If Edinger says that Hephaestus is required to have his feet on the ground for his creative potential to flourish, Chiron, on the other hand, has to humanize his pain, bringing it down to the mortal condition so it can be alleviated. Both Hephaestus and Chiron had to give up the Olympic prerogative to be realized in the concrete world.

The projection of creative power onto the lower limbs

Another aspect of the mark on the lower limb that needs to be considered is that it not only distinguishes the creative being, but it is also the place onto which the creative capability is projected. Quite often, a whole community projects onto an individual who bears the deformity, lesion, or even the absence of the lower limb, representing many of the transformative and liberating capabilities latent in the group.

Along with creativity, which is associated with the lower limbs, the biological aspect of creation, or sexuality, can also be contemplated in the semiotics of such limbs. Therefore, in this last section of Chapter 2, creativity, lower limbs, and sexuality will be discussed using several mythic narratives.

With the Otomis, in the central part of Mexico, shamanic activities were common among individuals who had lesions on their limbs. A missing limb in the images of different deities often indicated a hindrance in sexual identity, or was a representation of the capacity to cure and to transform. A Maya divinity named Cavil (*K'awill*), with great shamanic power, displayed a serpent in the place of its left foot (Figure 2.7). It is believed that this divinity was the first shamanic being and sorcerer, prior to Tezcatlipoca.

In general, physical deformities, including mutilation or loss of body segments, show a strong association with the phallic aspects of creativity, especially those related to the feet. Jung tells us that "*the foot . . . seems to possess a magic power of creation,*"[19] and enumerates different mythic characters with phallic aspect, that is, creativity. Ugliness as well as deformities also come along with creative trend among the chthonic gods. Jung emphasizes thid teluric quality by adding that "*the feet, being closer to the ground, represent, in dreams, a relation of earthy reality, and quite often have a generative or phallic meaning.*"[20]

The generative character of the feet can be observed in a great variety of myths within different cultures. In the Hindu pantheon, this phallic creative aspect of the foot is seen with a female deity, Yaksi. This nature goddess makes the sap flow from a tree trunk when she kicks her heel against it. She represents the natural power that drives the human being towards a more plenteous life. In Indian iconography, Shiva is often seen lying down, in a creative mood, while Lakshimi holds onto or massages his foot. It seems that the figure of a female consort acts as an "animation" so that the creative spirit or Shiva can generate

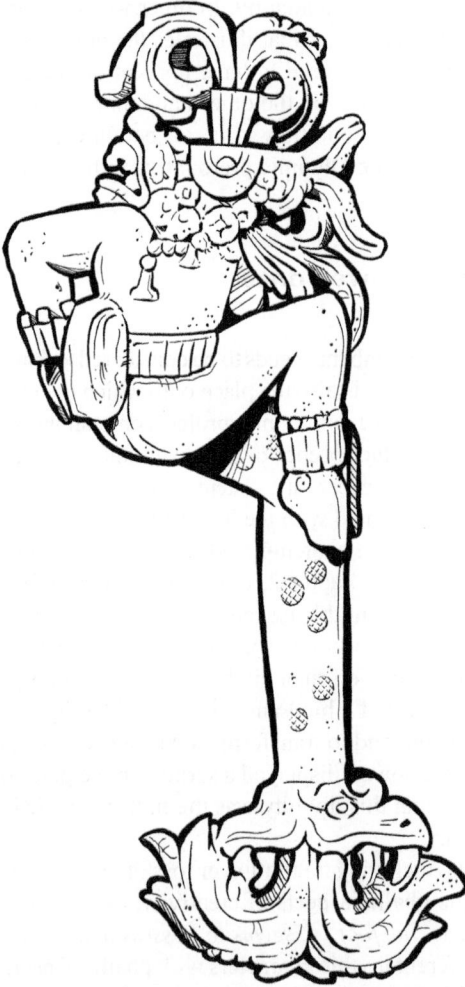

Figure 2.7 Drawing of the serpent-footed Maya goddess K'awill.

Brahma. When Bodhisattva ("he whose being is enlightenment") touches the ground with his feet, the flowers of diamonds and jewels spread out and cover everything in all directions.[21]

In a myth told by the Kamairuá, a Brazilian indigenous people, there is a being in the form of a wild dog that plays the flute. He rescues a little girl who had been abandoned by her mother because she could not stop crying. The wild dog raises her and then marries her. But now that she is a grown woman, a member of her former tribe finds her and impregnates her. He then starts threatening the wild dog, who flees into the woods with his flute. The wild dog resents abandonment, so he stamps his feet on the ground and all the surroundings turn into a dense forest again.[22]

In the mythology of another Brazilian native tribe, the Tupinambá, there is a story about two brothers, Aricoute and Tamendonare, who also illustrate the creative aspect of the feet. According to the legend, these two brothers are rivals with different temperaments. Aricoute despises his brother and considers him to be a coward. One day, Tamendonare humiliates his brother for having brought only the arm of an enemy as a trophy. Irritated, Aricoute throws the trophy against Tamendonare's hut, which immediately shoots up to the sky, taking the whole village with it. Tamendonare stamps his foot on the ground, making water spring up all over, and the water eventually covers the earth. The two brothers, with their wives, survive by climbing the trees, and later repopulate the earth. It is said that the Tupinambá tribe descends from Tamendonare and the Timinós from Aricoute.[23]

Among yet another Brazilian Indian tribe, the Munduruku (the tribe which supposedly extinguished the last of the Tapajó Indians), it is said that their Supreme Creator God, Caru Sacaebê, stamped his foot on the ground, opening up a cleft from where he brought forth a couple of each race: the Indians, the Blacks, the Whites and the Munduruku (since they are a race apart from the others).[24]

Stamping the foot on the ground is, therefore, a very prevalent symbol for creation, and involves both human feet as well as the feet of animals. In fairy tales, when horses kick a stone, it usually results in the appearance of a spring. Hippocrene, which literally means "horse-fountain," may be one of the best examples of this theme. In Greek mythology, the Fountain of the Muses was produced by a stroke of the hoof of Pegasus, thus bringing about poetic inspiration and creativity.

While this motif occurs among the Brazilian natives, in the Hindu pantheon, and in Mesoamerican and Greek lore, we can also observe it in the Muslim story of Ishmael, Abraham's rejected son, who was sent to the wilderness with his mother Hajar. After wandering lost in the dry desert and almost dying of thirst, Ishmael is said to have kicked the ground and then a spring began to flow. This spring, now called the Zamzam well, is located within Masjid al-Haram, in Mecca, Saudia Arabia, some steps east of the Kaaba, which is known as the holiest site in Islam. Stomping the foot and its association to procreativity seems to be considered even more seriously among the Muslims, as the Q'uran's Surah Al-Noor (24–31) states that women should refrain from striking their feet on the ground to avoid arousing desirousness in men.

The phallic and manly qualities of the feet can be appreciated in addition to the generative and creative aspects. For example, the Otomi word for "penis" (kwa) also means "foot," and it is curious to observe how often this phoneme entices a masculine trait across cultures: the San people in the Kalahari desert of Southern Africa utilize the word Kwai when referring to "man";[25] Hexagram 43 in the I Ching is called Kuai, meaning "resoluteness/breakthrough"; and the Korean expression *Kwae* is the principle of movement of objects and events. Thus, the absence of a foot or a lesion signaled an impairment of Otomi masculinity, as the foot was related to the penis. The archetypal character of the association between foot and masculinity can be seen in Brazil as well, since a lesbian woman is called *Sapatão*, which means "Big Shoe," for incorporating a masculine character while sexually relating to another woman.

Symbolically, the absence of feet or a lesion on the foot can be associated, therefore, with a compromise in man's masculinity since this limb is equated to the penis in different cultures. Among the Otomi, it was not uncommon for a male shaman to metamorphose himself into a woman by removing one of his legs. From a psychological standpoint, this conception is important as it points to the necessity to incorporate, or thoroughly live the opposite inside oneself, so that the totality of the psyche (the Self) can be realized. Different from King Nebuchadnezzar, who dreamt of a statue that had half-iron and half-clay feet, which only bears the opposites juxtaposed on himself, the Otomi shaman presents them as overlapping and mixed, so that a third entity can be made manifest.

As we can see, the feet have both a generative and a phallic character and the mark they bear reveals a being who is in possession of creative power. But it is also intriguing to observe that a lesion or even the absence of a limb is also associated with illicit sexual intercourse. However, this assumption is more likely to be found in the logic of archaic cultures where consciousness has not yet achieved the same level of sophistication that is observed within contemporary societies, and where the rationalization between cause and effect seems to be more direct and, not uncommonly, naïve. These cultures might conclude that whenever someone is born with an abnormality, it resulted from an illegitimacy. This assumption also implies that sound offspring resulted from a marital sexual relationship.

For instance, among the Nahua, physical deformities and many other disturbances in both individual and social lives were attributed to ambiguous sexual behavior and, therefore, in a way, were not fostered. However, it was believed that individuals who were born with these conditions were necessary to appease the terrible forces of nature during seasonal changes. Often times, the transition between the changes of season or astronomical periods were marked by cosmic terror, including fear of social chaos, physical and mental diseases, impotence, disorientation, and feminine infertility. All these terrors resulted in the loss of meaning in life. During these periods, the Nahuas worshiped divine beings that bore physical or sexual idiosyncrasies. It was also believed that such distortions gave form to those dangerous forces of nature and, by that, the Nahuas could contain these forces, transforming them into something new and positive. In this way, the signs that reflected an inversion of order were reverenced and sexual ambiguity and the physical deformities were the most worshiped on these occasions.

Another example can be seen among the Aztec, when a young girl was sacrificed in honor of the Cihuacoatl goddess as an atonement ritual between the dry and the rainy seasons. Cihuacoatl is a half-woman and half-serpent deity considered the first feminine being to give birth; therefore, she is thought of as the protector of those women who give birth and those women who die during the process. The celebrant would put on the sacrificed girl's clothes and hold out her decapitated head. After this, he would dance, kicking backwards, enacting the "inversion of order." By enacting this ritualistic dance, the Aztec counteracted the wrongdoing from the previous season.

A rite that was used to avert domestic evil, especially when food resources were scarce, consisted of leaving the house by walking backwards, with the feet turned back. This kind of walk was related to demonic powers, and it was believed that individuals born with their feet turned backwards (a club foot or *talipes equinovarus*) were children of unfaithful mothers. It was also believed that difficulties during pregnancy or at birth were related to transgressions in sexual behavior. Cihuateteo, the embodiment of five spirits of noble women who died during labor, was depicted with her feet turned backwards, signaling that she had been an adulteress. Symbolically, moving backwards indicates that we must turn our backs on conditions that were lived only superficially. Therefore, walking backwards is an opportunity to catch up contents that were not satisfactorily integrated.

In Aztec mythology, Xolotl is another important figure in the divine pantheon. According to the legend, he is a twin brother of Quetzalcoatl, the great god of creation. Quetzalcoatl is depicted as the feathered serpent, while Xolotl is depicted as a dog, and in some of the iconographies appears with his feet turned backwards. As a twin and brother of the Aztec solar god, Xolotl is master of the underworld; he protects the Sun during its nightly journey through the underworld, and is also the conductor of man on this journey, giving him the fire of wisdom. In addition, Xolotl serves as a psychopomp, and his reverse feet may allude to the process of return or resurrection of the souls of the dead, or even to the return of the Sun, indicating the reverse path to be taken. This re-creation of life may be contemplated every morning when Xolotl accompanies the Sun at night and delivers it soon after dawn.[26]

In Brazil, the mythic being with reverse feet is named Curupira—a boy with a furry body, red hair, and no outlets for his physiological functions, or no sexual organs (Figure 2.8).

However, the lack of certain physical attributes varies from one region to another. In some regions he is called Caapora and is depicted riding a wild boar, an animal usually associated with the feminine, as mentioned earlier. He is a demonic being who can do either good or evil, depending on how he is treated. His main task is to protect the forest, the newborn animals, and their mothers from unscrupulous hunters. Human beings avoid being harmed by the Curupira by offering him tobacco whenever they enter the forest. Curupira uses his inverse feet to trick trespassers in the woods; he is uncommonly strong and lethal, and his association with nature makes him a demonic entity linked to the feminine. In some places, he is celebrated on "Tree Day," or September 21 in Brazil.[27] Symbolically, Curupira represents a demoniac and destroying aspect of the psyche against an inflated and preying ego that has no consideration for the instinctive powers.

Figure 2.8 Curupira, drawing based on a sculpture made by Zema, a Brazilian clay-master.

Even though Curupira and Xolotl share the same reverse feet feature, their symbolic functions are distinct. The reverse feet of Curupira contribute to confuse and mislead a trespassing human being, while Xolotl's help in delivering the dead souls back to the light. Both of these figures are good examples of the dual aspect of the unconscious, which uses the same kind of allegory to signal different situations. When interpreting dreams, myths, or fairy tales, the image of reverse feet represents the impossibility of reducing the meaning of the symbol to a simple system of codes that can be easily accessed. Reverse feet can refer to the unconscious's tendency towards progress and growth (as in Xolotl) by showing the path of resurrection and acquisition of knowledge. But, as in Curupira, the symbol can also point to a regressive and destructive tendency if the human being acts in a way that is unrelated with nature.

One last psychological implication related to these mythic stories is that the deformity excludes the individual from the collective norm. This is an important point because, as Jung says, the great transformation can only occur in the individual. Only those who can step beyond mass psychology are more prone to experience the eternal dimension of the Self. In a symbolic way, an individual who is born with a physical deformity becomes "abnormal"; he or she does not fit in the collective patterns and, consequently, represents the differentiation needed to bear the transforming forces of the unconscious. Often, individuals who undergo psychotherapy report feeling like they are strangers to the people they have normally related to in the past. Once the analytical process enables the individual to become more differentiated, he or she often experiences the unconscious in a way that cannot be understood by collective or cultural norms.

Notes

1 Burland, C., & Forman, W. (1985). *The Aztecs*. Kranj: Gorenjski Tisk, Golden Press, p. 55.
2 Séjourné, L. (1970). *Pensamiento y religión en el México antiguo*. México: Fondo de Cultura Económica, p. 79.
3 Castro, E. V. (1986). *Araweté: Os deuses canibais*. Rio de Janeiro: Zahar, p. 184.
4 Jung, C. G., & McGuire, W. (1984). *Dream analysis: notes of the seminar given in 1928–1930*. Princeton, NJ: Princeton University Press, p. 134.
5 von Franz, M. (1997). *Archetypal patterns in fairy tales*. Toronto: Inner City Books, p. 97 ff.
6 Jung, C. G., Read, H., Fordham, M. S., & Adler, G. (1953–1979). *The collected works of C. G. Jung*. Princeton, NJ: Princeton University Press. *Symbols of Transformation*, CW 5, §450. (From now on, only Jung, C. G. (year) title CW volume, §.)
7 Willis, C. M, Church, S. M., Guest, C. M., et al. (2004). "Olfactory detection of human bladder cancer by dogs: proof of principle study." *British Medical Journal*, 329(7468): 712.
8 Klein, C. F., & Quilter, J. (2001). *Gender in pre-Hispanic America: a symposium at Dumbarton Oaks, 12 and 13 October 1996*. Washington, DC: Dumbarton Oaks Research Library and Collection, p. 201.
9 Edinger, E. F., & Wesley, D. A. (1994). *The eternal drama: the inner meaning of Greek mythology*. Boston, MA: Shambhala, p. 97 ff.
10 Frazer, J. G. (1976). The golden bough: a study in magic and religion. London: Macmillan, p. 578.
11 Frey-Rohn, L. (1990). From Freud to Jung: a comparative study of the psychology of the unconscious. Boston, MA: Shambhala, p. 275.
12 Jung, C. G. (1967). *Freud and psychoanalysis*, CW 4, § 469.
13 Neumann, E., & Manheim, R. (2015). *The Great Mother: an analysis of the archetype*. Princeton, NJ: Princeton University Press, p. 22.
14 Jung, C. G. (1979). *Symbols of transformation*, CW 5, § 351.
15 Vernant, J., & Vidal-Naquet, P. (2006). *Myth and tragedy in ancient Greece*. New York, NY: Zone Books, p. 115 ff.
16 Onians, R. B. (1973). *The origins of European thought*. New York, NY: Arno Press, p. 539.
17 Klein, C. F., & Quilter, J. (2001). *Gender in pre-hispanic America: a symposium at Dumbarton Oaks, 12 and 13 October 1996*. Washington, DC: Dumbarton Oaks Research Library and Collection, p. 235.
18 Edinger, E. F., & Wesley, D. A. (1994). *The eternal drama: the inner meaning of Greek mythology*. Boston, MA: Shambhala, p. 36.

19 Jung, C. G. (1979). *Symbols of transformation*, CW 5, § 450.
20 idem.
21 Campbell, J. (2017). *The hero with a thousand faces*. Mumbai: Yogi Impressions, p. 151.
22 Bôas, C. V., & Bôas, O. V. (1986). *Xingu*. Porto Alegre: Editora Kuarup, p. 141.
23 Métraux, A., Pinto, E., & Schaden, E. (1979). *A religião dos tupinambás: e suas relações com a das demais tribus tupi-guaranis*. São Paulo: Companhia Editora Nacional, p. 31.
24 Coudreau, H. (1977). *Viagem ao Tapajos*. Belo Horizonte: Itatiaia, p. 102.
25 Keane, A. H. (1896). *Ethnology: in two parts*. Cambridge: Cambridge University Press, p. 249.
26 Séjourné, L. (1970). *Pensamiento y religión en el México antiguo*. México: Fondo de Cultura Económica, p. 82.
27 Roque, C. (1968). *Grande enciclopédia da Amazônia*. Belém do Pará: Amazônia Ed., p. 781.

Chapter 3

The one-footedness

As seen in the previous chapters, there are several mythical narratives that can be analyzed as allegorical dispositions for various aspects related to the development of consciousness, especially regarding its dynamics to the unconscious. However, what has been discussed so far is infinitesimal given the countless stories that recount this interaction. This is because as consciousness integrates certain content, new contents are constellated in the unconscious. It might be said that a human being's fate is but to try to continuously accommodate the psychic flow of life. Needless to say, this condition requires a perennial exercise of creativity and transformation of the reality which has just been embraced.

Chapter 1 proposed a parallel between evolution in the form of locomotion and the process of development of consciousness, that is, the higher level of complexity in the dynamics of human consciousness coincides with a pattern of deambulation based exclusively on two limbs. It was also suggested that an even more sophisticated perception of reality, perhaps a "meta-reality," would be accompanied by a more specialized form of body support and mobility as seen in the symbolism of unipedalism or one-footedness.

If we return to the idea of phylogenetic development and consider it from a metaphoric point of view, we can see how the appearance of birds among the chordate animals preannounces a specialized representation of development in humankind. Birds, as well as human beings, count on bipedalism to move on the ground, although without achieving, in general, the psychic sophistication that can be observed among mammals or that can be compared to primates or humans. Nonetheless, the development of wings allowed the bird to navigate an aerial environment. Such a condition strongly appealed to human beings because these animals represent, symbolically, creatures that have the capability to transcend and visit ethereal kingdoms.

The growth of wings and bipedalism observed among birds can also be understood as a further development along the evolution scale that allowed these creatures to reach the pneumatic or "spiritual" milieu, and make use of this ambience in a more concrete way. In other words, birds do not only reside on the surface of the earth, but they can also reach the skies. From a human point of view, the pneumatic or "spiritual" kingdom can only be reached internally, that is, in a symbolical way. Concretely, however, such a domain may be reached by means of planes or space shuttles that have been created by man in order to allow him to fly. Thus, when we encounter images of individuals standing on only one limb, this refers us back to a possibility of visiting the world beyond or a transcendentalized condition. The images of unipedalism, be they anthropomorphic or mythological allegory, therefore, should not be considered only as a physical handicap. Rather, they can be viewed as symbolic images of one who is capable of a "transitus" between the conscious and the unconscious realms and who has the potentiality to unite the opposing dispositions which have been split apart.

Earlier, when the association between lower limbs and cosmogony was discussed, we looked at the myth of Tezcatlipoca, who had to leave one of his feet in the realm of the unconscious, in the mouth of Tlaltecuhtli, the Great Caiman. While with one foot the god remained within the unconscious, with the other he transited in the world of humankind. Thus, Tezcatlipoca became an intermediator god between humankind and the other gods.

In Brazil, we also have a one-legged being called Saci-Pererê (Figure 3.1). He is usually depicted as a naked, young black boy, smoking a pipe, and wearing only a red beret. He has a hole in each of his palms, through which he manages to carry brazing charcoal without burning himself. Because he appears in a culture that is already established, the cosmogonic character, in the strict sense of the word, cannot be ascribed to him. However, he might also be considered a creator of a higher moral conscience in our culture. Saci is rather mercurial and, among his various features, his ability to deceive stands out, which in principle does not allow man to forget his own limitations, imperfections, and idiosyncrasies. Saci represents disorder, a lack of harmony, and an incredible dose of humor in all things he does (at least from his own perspective). He heralds our deviations in conduct, and somehow mirrors our limitations. He carries our faults and, under this perspective, signals our need to assimilate those imperfections. While Tezcatlipoca lost his foot due to the battle for the creation of humankind and in its place substituted the obsidian mirror to show the limitations of the human race, Saci, on the other hand, hops on one foot, reflecting the difficulty of a complete separation between consciousness and the unconscious processes. Sometimes, depending on the region, Saci is also called Matinta-Perê and is depicted as a bird of bad omen. As a bird, he corroborates the idea of free transit between different realms.

Upon visiting us, Saci leaves one leg in the metaphorical "jaws of the unconscious" and shows us that we are still deeply bonded to its constructive or destructive powers. His duty is to remind us about the incompleteness of our consciousness, no matter how hypertrophic it may seem to be. It is possible that Saci also had to fight a heroic battle to free himself from the deep shadows of the unconscious and, from time to time, causes an impression on our daily routine. He emerges from the unconscious in his paradoxical characteristic manner, since

Figure 3.1 Saci-Pererê (Monteiro Lobato, with permission from Álvaro Gomes).

he puts unexpectedness and confusion side by side with apparently orderly situations. Therefore, he must have attempted to separate from the unconscious with exactly this purpose, that is, to reflect our miseries so as to forge their integration.

The figure of Saci, however, no longer plays an important part as a transformative symbol in Brazilian culture these days. Instead, he is more often viewed as an emblematic folkloric figure, and his appeal is much weaker as a living force in the collective unconscious. There are no serious followers of Saci who fear, favor, or pay him honor. Instead, he has become part of a TV series that has satirized and deprived him of his powers. He has lost his numinous feature, and with it his divine attribution to be a receptacle of human maladies. Saci seems to have died as an image. However, it is still amazing to observe how strongly his "presence" can be felt. We Brazilians might not name the "pranks" that we have to deal with daily as Saci's ordeals, but we can definitely feel the immense collective shadow we have not integrated in our political, economic, social, or personal affairs.

If we consider the rationale of unipedalism, the images of lameness might then be seen as an indication of some kind of advantage or as an ability for realization. For example, the one-legged dance the shaman carries out can be understood as his capacity to keep his support in two distinct domains; a condition similar to Saci. However, Saci is a being who belongs to the "other" world and appears furtively when least expected, and the shaman is a being who belongs to "this world," mastering the power over the hidden forces of the magic world, which allows him to move freely between both worlds.

While the ontogenetical evolution of human beings is marked by bipedalism, it seems that, symbolically, unipedalism amounts to a differentiating factor in the individual as far as psychological development is concerned. Once unipedalic beings are acquainted with the reality from both here and "there," assumedly they are more equipped to make better judgments, follow a road of lesser conflicts, and develop reconciling attitudes. In other words, someone who is one-footed conveys the idea of being less prone to fastening or identifying himself with a unilateral view of life. The lack of virtue in being two-footed could then be ascribed to clinging to a point of view (getting stuck with an idea), thus losing the notion of relativism. In Portuguese there are expressions, such as *fincar o pé* ("to dig in one's heel") or *não arredar o pé* ("move not the foot"), which indicate a person who is very much identified with his or her own idea. These are people who are stuck in their opinions and, paradoxically, are fairly immobile. That is why, when Yahweh dislocated Jacob's hip, it meant that from that moment on he would have to adopt a different manner with which to progress his life.

In this way, images of unipedalism can be viewed as an advanced allegory for the symbolical development of the psychic processes. Figure 3.2 is a particular representation among several bizarre images alchemists made to express their inner search for meaning. The alchemists often made use of strange words or expressions to emphasize the extraordinary nature of an object. One of these expressions is "monocolus" (uniped).

As an image, the uniped is not so strange, as already demonstrated in the aforementioned myths, although the message it conveys is not usual. Jung informs us that the "stone" is described as a monocolus in more than one alchemical text. In the codex of Abraham the Jew, for example, there is a picture of two one-footed kings bound together like Siamese twins. These two similar images convey the idea of the "duality in unity of Mercurius and to the coming into consciousness of the opposites," which is one of the aspects of the *coniunctio*.[1]

Figure 3.2 Monocolus.

Expressed by the image of the monocolus, this idea of uniting the opposites can also be seen in the Mesoamerican Otomi ritual where the missing lower limb renders a man feminine.[2] In both the alchemical description and in this ritual, there is an "indication of complementarity between '*physis*' and spirit" which must be reunited as the first step of the *coniunctio*, or *unio mentalis*.[3] In this stage, soul and spirit must be united with the body, which on a personal level must be understood as the ego personality coming to terms with its shadow. In other words, the *unio mentalis* is the knowledge of oneself. As an example, Jung cites St. Simeon Stylites, who stood on one leg upon a pillar for seven years as a demonstration of the possibility of communion between spirit and the body.[4]

Thus, by knowing oneself better as conveyed by the monocolus, it means that a higher level of consciousness has been achieved; soul, spirit, and body are acquainted on a mental level. We may read the same idea in an Arab alchemical manuscript (*The Twelve Chapters by Ostanes the Philosopher on the Philosopher's Stone*) attributed to Ostanes, where, in his struggle to deepen his consciousness, he says:

> I am going to set out for you the allegory of the body, the vital spirit, and the soul [i.e. soma, pneuma, psyche]. Study it with your reason and your intelligence, and, if you give it all your attention, you will be set well on your way to accomplish each work and to learn all that is hidden.[5]

With Ostanes, it may seem a little easier to bring the concept of *unio mentalis* into reality since he is more explicit in saying that the triad union is to be accomplished by intelligence or reasoning. In other words, it is by means of conscious effort that this realization takes place. By pneuma he conveys the idea of something in every person that links the body-soul with the living universe, whereas the soul is that which activates the body and enables it, through the pneuma, to achieve universality. Once the body is penetrated by the soul, this mixture favors the joining of pneuma, which establishes a new and active relationship to the cosmos. Soul is then what brings light to the darkness of the body, while the spirit is that which universalizes the triad altogether, making "it" known.

This new acquaintance may be expressed, for example, by the extra knowledge obtained by the Otomi shaman. Jung also mentions the myth of Isis and Osiris to clarify this idea. Isis copulates with the spirit of the dead Osiris, and from this union comes Harpokrates, the god of mystery. In this myth, Isis represents the soul, Osiris is the spirit, and Osiris's corpse the body. The state of *unio mentalis* is then completed by the begetting of Harpokrates. Etymologically, Harpokrates means "weak in the lower limb,"[6] an allegory that has been expanded into other idiosyncrasies to convey a similar condition, that is, lameness akin to a higher level of achievement of consciousness.

In practical terms, the state of *unio mentalis* may be better appreciated when we look at the ways in which individuals relate to their dreams. It is not uncommon that people have wonderful dreams that may carry a deep revealing potential of personal mystery, although they may not always reach the preannounced epiphany. For such a realization, though, it would be necessary that the dream, as an aspect of pneuma, be lodged in an animated *physis*. That is, it requires an individual who has moved towards self-knowledge by doing the laborious work with his or her own shadow material that would otherwise be projected externally. Only then can the spirit penetrate and reveal the universal truth of the Self. Thus, it is only with the effort of the intellect and the wish to understand (reasoning), as pointed out by Ostanes, that the "knowledge of what is hidden" may be unveiled.

Following the same theme of the monocoli, there are other mythical images that also register this transcendental prerogative. For example, there are representations of individuals with one eye or one tooth, or others like Melampus (black foot), Oedipus (Swollen Foot), and Hermes (in his ithyphallic depiction) that also convey the idea of penetrating and revealing what is hidden. The image of the uniped stands for that which is capable of uniting the opposites at a higher level, engendering that which is mysterious. It is worth mentioning that the *unio mentalis* is only the beginning of the union; the engendered "mysterium" must be realized back into the *physis*, into concreteness. That's why the shaman must do his work within the community; otherwise he will get sick. Similarly, when an individual has a revealing dream and integrates it mentally, but gives no practical application to it, nor brings it to realization into life as the image may have suggested, the dream becomes worthless. This is also what is meant by integration of a psychic content, that is, to give a human dimension to an archetypal reality.

When we think about integration, the image of Shiva's dance inside a circle of fire—where he is standing on his right foot while pointing with his left hand to his left foot suspended in the air—also comes to mind as a union of opposites. The purpose of the dance is the release of an illusory idea of ego supremacy and the giving up of the physical world. In addition, Shiva's dance symbolically represents the necessity of a deep integration, within a human being, of the contents of experience, both physical and spiritual. This integration must take place without our becoming lost or, psychologically speaking, by not identifying ourselves with any of the domains. So, we can see that Shiva lifts himself up but keeps his right foot on the back of Natesa, the demon of mundane affairs. In this image, it seems that the *unio mentalis* is an entelechy in the human psyche, as if the urge for integration of opposites is an innate condition.

A further example of this urge may be examined in the marble votive relief related to the sanctuary of Blaute (Figures 3.3 and 3.4).[7]

At the top is an image of a sandal with the sole and strips of leather or metal. The sole shows the drawing of a supplicant in adoration. The largest part of the relief is occupied by a snake in an ascending movement. The inscription carved between the snake and the sole, which continues to the left of the relief, refers to the one who dedicated the piece of work, Silon (around 350 BCE). At a first glance, we might understand this image to be an *ex voto*, a religious offering, by someone who had been bitten by a snake and was saved from death. However, symbolically speaking, we can also consider it as an allegory of the contents hidden in the unconscious that seek understanding or try to approach a human point of view, as we discussed earlier with the Garden of Eden. When we consider that the "human point of view" is not represented by a two-footed equivalent in this votive relief, but only by the left foot, then it is probable that this image points to a further integration. Perhaps the ascending movement of the serpent towards the left side of someone who is in a devotional attitude could indicate that the great

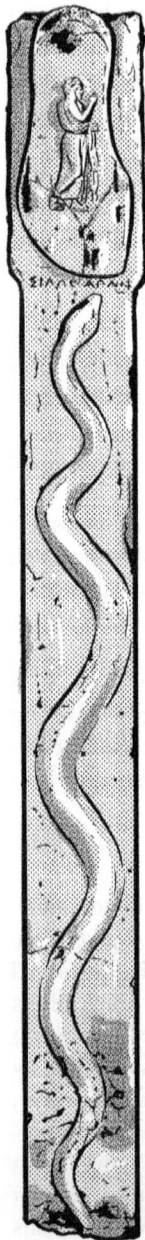

Figures 3.3 and 3.4 Hero on Blaute (drawing based on a votive plate c. 350 BC, Acropolis Museum).

union of a human being with the chthonic primeval powers can only be attained with one's "left" side, or introspection.

This image further suggests that both introversion and devotion are necessary conditions to achieve the state of *unio mentalis*, so that "what is hidden in *physis* by projection is made conscious."[8] In psychological terms, one who has been poisoned and becomes cured moves from a state of nigredo to a deliverance towards the spiritual (understanding) domain. It is a condition that can be seen when one is no longer a prisoner of the mundane existence represented by the intense functioning of the ego in its too discriminatory and strong standpoint (as is suggested by Shiva's one foot on the back of Natesa). It seems that the *unio mentalis* is an entelechy present in the human psyche, as if the union of opposites is an inborn condition, which we must struggle to achieve in our lifetime.

As with any symbolic material, each analysis of a given allegory cannot exclude its other side, the opposite that it fatally constellates. Thus, we must consider what the opposite might be in our discussion of the monocolus. Psychologically, the great danger with unipedalism is that it could convey the idea that an individual may lack a robust base of support when compared with a two-footed stand. With a one-footed posture the individual has a less realistic anchoring to one's ideas or judgments. In practical terms, shamans are often perceived as strange and are usually avoided and feared by the members of the community because of their eccentricities. Quite often, they live a reclusive life, very different from their community, and do not always engage in the general life of the culture. Therefore, it is necessary that the individual who has one foot on the earth is conscious enough about where the other foot could be stepping in the beyond. If unipedalism suggests an ascension, then it also bears the possibility of losing reality, a lack of materiality, or the absence of a robust base of support as its shadow.

In Plato's *Symposium*, the uniped image is a reference to both the hubris and the punishment that is caused by the identification with such states of hyperconsciousness, that is, with the gods. Plato presents a myth in which the primordial being contains in itself both male and female genders, as well as the union of them. These primeval beings were round, had four hands and four feet, and their backs and sides formed a circle. But, because of their power, they wanted to approach Olympus, and ended up attacking the gods. As a punishment for their daring act, Zeus split them apart and cursed them to search for their other half for the rest of their existence. Now separated from one another, man and woman each wander on two legs in search of his or her other half. Zeus then threatens them further: "if they continue with their insolence and do not be quiet, I will cut them off again, so that they will have to hop on just one leg."[9]

Other images of creatures similar to the monocolus were utilized in medieval Christian lore to represent the forbidden land (the demon's land). These mythological beings with only one leg were called Sciapods, which etymologically means "shadow feet." It was said that they belonged to tribes of one-legged Ethiopian or Indian men who had a single giant foot that they raised in the air to shade themselves against the hot southern sun. These images were popular in medieval bestiaries and map illustrations of the Terra Incognita, and were utilized to frighten people off those lands. In the Middle Ages, anything that was not yet Christianized was considered evil. The Sciapods, as well as many other monstrosities, represented the Church's fear of the unknown world beyond, which was, of course, inhabited by the devil. Psychologically, it is interesting to note that the "shadow foot" is the interface between that which is known (consciousness) and that which is feared and unknown (unconsciousness). But even more ironical is the pictorial representation of the big foot, which is utilized as protection from the heat of the tropical sunlight (clarity/consciousness).[10] It seems that the Sciapods offer another allegory for the sectarianism of the Christian world as far as the "world of darkness," or the unconscious, is concerned.

*∗∗

Up to this point, we can see that many amplifications have been utilized to emphasize the symbolic role of lower limbs as far as psychic expansion is concerned. These limbs, in each of their segments, carry a chiaroscuro quality, that is, they have both a progressive and a regressive aspect, meaning that they can either corroborate or contradict a given assertion. If, for example, a lesion or a mark on a limb constellates a deficiency or social discrimination, it also points to specialization, or the possibility of realizing uncommon tasks.

When we consider the previous examples in the context of psychic development, we can see the impressive association with the lower limbs and the feminine. In this respect, the creative movement akin to the lower limbs harbors within the feminine the "vanishing point" in practically all of its manifestations. Independent of the way the feminine presents itself—as earth, water, woman, mother, anima, or even the unconscious itself—the fact is that everything departs from and converges into such a point, as if it were a Renaissance painting. There are times when it is necessary to sever the relationship to the feminine for the sake of differentiation and knowledge; but there are also situations when it is imperative to return to it, to revisit or unite with the feminine again so that new life can emerge.

To know who or what is in charge of the evolution seems to be an unanswerable, yet intriguing, question. Was it the progressive acquisition of bipedalism that led to a higher level of consciousness, or was it the ongoing development in consciousness that allowed the living being to change from sliding along on the ground and in the water to a two-footed or one-footed stand? Maybe these two aspects are parallel, so that any advance in one is borrowed and improved upon by the other, and vice versa. And, it might be most important to acknowledge this association between both aspects, as one surely corroborates and modifies the other.

Another aspect we can derive from the material presented so far is that the great common denominator to all these processes is the "mood of creativity" that the lower limbs bring about. In our quest for consciousness, humankind had to be creative enough to master the movement to and from the feminine/unconscious. As human beings, we must rely on our impressive capability to transform the vicissitudes we come across during this journey, whether it's dealing with the "waters of life," finding new strategies, reversing the order of the natural elements, healing a hampering wound, tricking the trickster, or uniting the opposing forces. As far as a new conscious attitude is concerned, the lower limbs stand for the symbolic locus of creativity in the body.

The lower limbs constantly offer us new opportunities in the process of acquiring new consciousness, sometimes, in the least expected way. For example, when I first started writing this book, I tore the muscle in my left calf while I was exercising. I knew, in a way, that I was approaching a subject that was rather relevant to my psyche. The previous week, as I was discussing the issues of the knee and making connections with the monocolus content, I sustained a more serious injury, this time in my left knee. I limped for quite some time afterwards and had to keep a bandage around my knee so as to get a better base of support. While moving around like this, I experimented with feeling like a uniped. I tried to understand what would be the symbolic meaning of this injury, since it happened in a rather unexpected and implausible way. What, then, could be the meaning of this "accident" at this very moment?

The body, as an objectified element for the gravid disposition of the psychic, is a receptacle of several cosmogonic representations in its various segments. For instance, beyond the images of creation that are projected on it, the knee also etymologically carries the idea of engendering. That is, both the image of and the idea related to creation can be associated with the knees.

An example of this on a primordial scale is the creation myth of the Tukuna people, a Brazilian Indian tribe. According to this myth, the chief called Natupá is stung by the Caba (wasps) on both knees, where later a tumor forms. The first two couples are born out of this tumor, and thus the whole Tukuna tribe.[11] The same motif of the creation of the first human being out of a swollen knee can also be observed in a cosmogenic African myth where a secondary divinity, called Ndorobo, gives birth to the first human from his swollen knee.[12]

In Latin, the composition element for the word "knee" is *genu-us,* which became vulgarized into its diminutive form as *geniculum,* and spread throughout the Romanic languages to designate "knee" as *ginocchio* (Italian), *genou* (French), and *joelho* (Portuguese). *Genu* also composes the word *genuínus* (meaning "innate, native, authentic"), a word that is synonymous with *ingennus. Ingennus,* however, comes from *gen,* from whence words such as *gender, genealogy,* and *generation* derived. The word "knee" also comes from *gónu* (Greek), which is a cognate for *génos* (meaning "race, generation, family"), and for *gígnomai* ("to be born"). So, not only is the image of the knee associated with creation, but the vocable itself is also related to creation, from both the Greek and the Latin origins. In ancient times there was a ritual where the child was only recognized as being a legitimate—or a *genuine*—son after his father had put him on his knees.[13] For the Indo-European people, the knees were also considered the locus for paternity, life, and the generation of power.[14] In a way, metaphorically speaking, the knees are to men what the womb is to women.

The fact that the knee brings together both the image and the idea of creation makes it function as a strong hook for such projections. This may also be related to the fact that the knees are the bodily segment which, paradoxically, releases one from being subservient to the divine, since a human being stands up and elevates one's stature through the knees. When a man or a woman (animals) stands up and walks about in this position, they face the image of the creator with a new disposition. It is not without reason, however, that any time humans recognize their own frailty—littleness—and need divine help, they must fold the knees again (that is the paradox!). Time and again, human beings must reconsider their hubris, their too-high standards, and bend down to what is superior.

I knew that what was injured in my knee was the patella, a segment of the lower limbs I had overlooked. Technically speaking, I had a patellar subluxation. When I began writing this book, I had thought about this bone, but did not give too much attention to it. Besides, I could not find any legend, fairy tale, or myth that offered symbolical support. But my patella did not want to be ignored! Biomechanically speaking, the function of the patella is to increase the amount of the torque made available by the muscles of the thigh. It achieves this by increasing the lever arm of the quadriceps, that is, the distance from the muscle to the axis of the knee, thus enhancing the mechanical advantage, its momentum.[15] Metaphorically, the patella "extracts" strength from the quadriceps.

From the evolutionary perspective, the patella is not universally present among vertebrates; fish, amphibians, reptiles, and birds do not develop this bone. Among mammals, a rather rustic bone called the sesamoid bone develops that is equivalent to the quadriceps muscle tendon. However, the patella in a human knee is much larger and thicker and moves into a position directly above the joint line when the knee is fully extended. This morphology allows a much larger tension to be built in the quadriceps, which then allows human beings to be in an upright position. It follows that a human being is the only animal capable of assuming a completely erect posture because of the function of the patella.

The word "patella" is also associated with an agricultural Roman goddess whose name is Patella (at other times Patana, Patelena, or Patellana). She is sometimes referred as a variation of Ceres or even as Ceres's daughter. As Patelena, she presides over the opening of husks of grains. As Patellana or Patella, she calls the grain to come forth and presides over it when it comes to light.[16]

Etymologically, *patella* means "a small plate," usually utilized in sacrifice rituals. The small dish a Catholic priest raises towards the sky with the Host on it is called a *paten*, a word that shares the same root as *patella*. It seems that both the patella bone and the goddess Patella have to do with the extraction of something; the former "extracts" strength, and the latter "extracts" the food and is also associated with a sacrificial act.

While the knees are mostly analyzed for the symbolic aspect concerned with creativity, we cannot bypass the idea that they can also be seen as the body segment *par excellence*, through which a human shows the deepest humbling countenance when facing the gods—the *genoflexorum*. Therefore, the idea of submission should be considered along with creation, and this is something that I had overlooked in my endeavor to investigate the lower limbs. In a way, this was a naïve omission considering the wound I had in my knee. It is always mandatory that an individual bend down on one's knees whenever beholding the divine!

If, however, the biomechanical relationship between the patella and knee is analyzed symbolically, it may convey something rather different. By kneeling, one is not only lowering one's stature—we might say "keeping a lower profile"—but is also offering one's geniality and frank creativity while facing God. Thus, an individual transforms oneself into an offering to the divine, since the patella is the plate that holds the bent knee (the *genium*) as if they both were the dish and the sacrificial offer respectively.

In an unpublished manuscript, Margret Ostrovski-Sachs writes about her conversations with Jung and records Jung's experience of fracturing his fibula in 1943. In his description, we can see that there is always a price to be paid whenever one is unconscious of the numinosity of given content:

> Jung comments that breaking his fibula was highly symbolic. He asked himself whether he was guilty of some sort of inflation that he was not aware of. He was willing to accept this possibility, and wished that someone could have told him so. But, after a while, he realized himself what was going on with him. He said he was on a foreign territory; it is as if you go hopping around the garden at night and suddenly fall down a hole. You do not notice it when you are on a foreign territory. It just happens to you but you get inflated because of it; and not knowing has the same effect as guilt. By that time he was writing about the anima and animus and had thought that he was just pursuing his interest in psychology. But he realized that he had moved into foreign territory; into God's country. Alchemy seemed to him to be an honorable scientific pursuit but its contents – the anima, the animus, the Self, the chymical marriage – they were transcendent realities and not just scientific concepts. They are gods! Jung said he did not know this, not because of some kind of pretentious ignorance, but rather out of naive foolishness, like Parsifal.

Jung seemed to have achieved a deeper understanding of what he had been investigating in a manner which, initially, appeared to be quite pragmatic. If, in the beginning, he was eagerly tackling the material based on a scientific, ego-like approach, the unconscious forced him to "break his sustentation" in order to become more conscious about the divine nature of the subject. Jung's fracture, or the limitation imposed to a lower limb, might be viewed as a hint to change the line of thought towards a broader understanding of a given content. It can also be considered as the lapidarian work of the unconscious towards consciousness. If Jung were Brazilian, in this situation, we could say that Saci had made himself present and, in Jung's case, the trickster's message was heard.

When I consulted the I Ching on the situation surrounding the conditions of this injury in my patella, it yielded Hexagram 61, the "Inner Truth." The initial statement reads:

> The wind blows over the lake and stirs the surface of the water. Thus visible effects of the invisible manifest themselves . . . The character of *fu* ("truth") is actually the picture of a bird's *foot* [emphasis mine] over a fledgling. It suggests the idea of brooding.

The image offered by the I Ching conveyed a deep call for introspection in the hope that an inner truth may be retrieved. The second changing line of the hexagram reinforced this idea:

> The crane need not show itself on a high hill. It may be quite hidden when it sounds its call; yet its young will hear its note, will recognize it and give answer. Where there is a joyous mood, there a comrade will appear to share a glass of wine.[17]

Perhaps, in this way, the wound in my patella may be, indeed, pointing to the fact that the contemplation of this territory requires a reverential and less active approach. Time is necessary so that those contents can be brooded.

Notes

1 Jung, E., Franz, M. V., & Dykes, A. (1998). *The Grail legend.* Princeton, NJ: Princeton University Press, p. 212.
2 Klein, C. F., & Quilter, J. (2001). *Gender in pre-Hispanic America: a symposium at Dumbarton Oaks, 12 and 13 October 1996.* Washington, DC: Dumbarton Oaks Research Library and Collection, p. 234.
3 Jung, C. G. (1970). *Mysterium coniunctionis,* CW 14, § 663 ff.
4 Jung, C. G., & Douglas, C. (1997). *Visions: notes of the seminar given in 1930–1934 by C. G. Jung* (Vol. 2). Princeton, NJ: Princeton University Press, p. 775.
5 Lindsay, J. (1970). *The origins of alchemy in Graeco-Roman Egypt.* London: Muller, p. 148.
6 Jung, C. G. (1979). *Symbols of transformation,* CW 5, § 356.
7 Elderkin, G. W. (1941). The hero on a sandal. *Hesperia, 10*(4), 381.
8 Jung, C. G. (1970). *Mysterium coniunctionis,* CW 14, § 722.
9 Meier, C. A. (1995). *Personality: the individuation process in the light of C. G. Jung's typology.* Einsiedeln: Daimon, p. 98.
10 Sekules, V. (2001). *Medieval art.* Oxford: Oxford University Press, p. 12.
11 Carvalho, S. M. (1979). *Jurupari: estudos de mitologia brasileira.* São Paulo: Editora Atica, p. 174.
12 Franz, M. V., & Franz, M. V. (1995). *Creation myths.* Boston, MA: Shambhala, p. 257.
13 Oliveira, F. R. (2006). Gesto e abstração: usos do verbo gounoûmai em Homero. *Trans/Form/Ação, 29*(1), 63–68.

14 Onians, R. B. (1973). *The origins of European thought*. New York, NY: Arno Press, p. 491.
15 Herzmark, M. (1938). The evolution of the knee joint. *Journal of Bone & Joint Surgery*, *20*(1): 77–84.
16 Leland, C. G. (1892). *Etruscan roman remains in popular tradition*. London: T. Fisher Unwin, p. 233.
17 Wilhelm, R. (Trans.), & Baynes, C. F. (Trans.) (1968). *The I Ching or book of changes: the Richard Wilhelm translation*. London: Routledge & Kegan Paul.

Chapter 4

An image materialized

The psychological interpretation of mythologems is not the kind of task that satisfies our intellect since we can hardly, if ever, reach a final conclusion about their contents. Considering that myths, fairy tales, sagas, and similar stories emulate varied but specific questions, the interpretative work will always be faulty or incomplete, especially because the questions they bring in are so vast and varied. Besides that, the interpretation is in constant danger of getting lost in itself, and not reaching the appropriate integration of the images because of the myriad aspects that could be attributed to a given symbol.

Quite often, the attempt to understand a given image may further be jeopardized by the lack of information or references about the material. There are certain conditions in which the thing to be analyzed is but a fragment, a piece, or an isolated image. Sometimes even the authorship or the time the material was produced cannot be verified, and much less what was the motivation behind the creation. Nonetheless, as far as psychology is concerned, what one is trying to achieve is to understand the symbolic meaning of that fragment or content which, in final analysis, is the expression of the unconscious. Therefore, the deficiency of objective information on any of these "images" may be eventually circumvented by analyzing the different modes of expression of analog images across cultures and historical times in their distinct and various manifestations.

As previously mentioned, Jung proposed the method of adducing correlate material from parallel sources in order to subsidize the understanding of a symbolic theme, and called it amplification. Without this method, one runs the risk of imprisoning certain content into previous and established concepts, which will mostly encase it into a presupposition rather than propitiate new knowledge. By comparing and contrasting analogous material to this "new image," we might avoid a reductionist view. In a way, the use of comparative themes allows the material to speak by itself. Every time a given image appears, whether it is in a same culture or even across cultures, no matter the context, it means that this image carries, in each moment it was utilized, one specific representation of the collective unconscious.

Therefore, when we transculturally study the various manifestations of a given image, or in other words when we amplify that image, we are acknowledging what is possible to be engendered by it, from the point of view of the unconscious. It is also important that, while we are trying to grasp the symbolical meaning of a given theme, we embrace all places it might have manifested, such as in popular music, fine arts, rituals, religious ceremonies, or oneiric material. Jung's method of amplification is, therefore, endowed with the possibility to enrich a given image with parallel material, and yet he warned that it should never be considered a closed system from which inflexible conclusions can be drawn that preclude new argumentations. The amplification is, in its essence, a heuristic method. Once it allows a progressive scrutiny over themes that belong to different groups of people or specific cultures in distinct periods of history, the interpretative endeavor opens up even more space so that the unconscious can be revealed in its proteanic and genuinely symbolic character.

It would not be incorrect to say that the discussions presented in Chapter 3 include, indeed, a vast amount of symbolic amplification of the "lower limbs" theme, brought about by dreams and bodily intercurrences as reported by analysands. Even if one may feel that such an enterprise may have been too excessive as far as the presentation and interpretations of images are concerned, as well as their associations, such an effort, nonetheless, is still incomplete and unsatisfactory. This is true since each analysis may invite a new interpretation to be carried on in its opposing sense, as always happens with symbolic material.

In a way, we might be concerned about harvesting so much material lest it not find a way to be appropriately processed. However, the unconscious appears to support such an attempt, as can been seen by the dream I had as I pondered this question:

> I was walking by the edge of a lake whose shore was surrounded by black earth. It was supposed to be where the Tapajó Indians used to live. I knew that I should keep my eyes open because it was possible that I could still see some mummies which might have been naturally unearthed there. I thought, or rather fantasized, that maybe some Indians might have been killed there and their bodies would come up to the surface of the mud. But I could not find anything. Then I stepped into the water and my foot reached a big hole and I fell in it. It was very deep and I felt that there were things there; maybe ancient icons, ceramics, and so forth. However, I did not have enough breath-holding capacity to investigate the place. So I was planning to get some diving material to come back and explore the place.

The emphasis of the black earth was very pertinent considering that Santarém, the region from where the Tapajoara statuette and the majority of the found archeological material come, has soil with this characteristic. Even today, several studies are still being made there because this region is part of the place where the Tapajó inhabited. According to archeologists, these people chose to live there because the earth was (is) very fertile. Therefore, from a psychic point of view, the dream suggests that I am stepping on "fecund" soil. I am aware, though, that I need some instrument or a method and even more strength to further enhance my ability to breathe into this material. It cannot be taken in with one single breath, as a matter of speaking. Notwithstanding, there are still things to be found! This dream also points out that I step in a hole and fall into the question I am searching for. Again, here is an image of my feet conducting me, or leading me, towards that which I have been called. And more importantly, the dream tells me that there are even more things to be understood.

In a Jungian analytic process, it would not be possible, or fair, to map out the analysands' questions concerning such bodily segments only in their semiotic aspects. This would congeal, restrict, obstruct, and cut off the psychic vital flow, causing a hindrance to the process of self-knowledge. Besides moving towards possible ways of understanding that which could be emulated from the available analogous material, it is necessary to make room for such symbols to express themselves. It was under this assumption that the Tapajoara statuette (the girl with her big toe in her mouth) joined each analytic discussion, inviting both analyst and analysand to pursue her aesthetics through a Jungian perspective.

The statuette was not the primary object of investigation of this work. However, when we consider all the discussions and reflections about the lower limbs that were going on with each analysand, its remarkable iconographic representation opened up a new lode to be explored. She was not only discussed for comparative purposes, but also as an object that needed to be investigated on her own value. When she appeared in the analytical sessions, it was as if a new dream was being reported. And it was under this premise that the invitation to discuss her features was put forth. Since there is no strong material to support anything that could be affirmed about her, any attempt to extract meaning out of her could not prescind from the comparative road; that is, from amplification.

Pragmatically speaking, this task is, obviously, quite daring and potentially inglorious once it can take you anywhere. Maybe we will never know for sure what this image may have meant to the Tapajó population or who molded it; whether it belonged to a ritual ceremony or if it were just a decorative object or only the result of some ceramist's play in his or her spare time. What matters now, though, is to try to come as close as possible to what this image might add, psychologically speaking, to the contemporary human being. Whether someone is Brazilian or from any other nation in the world, we are now facing a powerful image. So, the question arises: What to do with her?

So far, we have examined the lower limbs, and more so the feet, as teleological organs *par excellence*, since their purpose is to take us, humans, somewhere else from whence we stand. There is, then, metaphorically speaking, a finality in the lower limbs. But what can be said about a stomapod (from Greek: *stoma* = mouth, and *podos* = foot) such as this Tapajoara icon? Even though this mystery is virtually impossible to answer, the next part of this chapter will bring together several considerations of analog iconographies and motifs in an attempt to contextualize this Tapajoara piece of art. Similar to dream interpretation, this is a kind of work to extract meaning out of the unconscious, so that consciousness can be fostered.

Tracking the statuette

It is challenging to understand this feminine anthropomorphic figure with her left foot in her mouth for different reasons. In former times, this statuette was buried together with many other pieces of ceramic artwork in a common pit by local people in the Amazon region of what is today the city of Santarém in the state of Pará in the northern part of Brazil. This city was built over the place where the Tapajó tribe once lived, and some of these relics have eventually been found by local people in their backyards.

Because of the European catechesis imposed by the Catholic priests, the local inhabitants were taught to fear and to adjure the "demonic" character of any indigenous artifact that was formerly utilized for worship in the community. The population was then instructed to destroy all these "devilish objects." But while the natives began to respect the Christian divinities, they also feared destroying the old images and icons because they knew they would be offending the other gods who belonged to their ancestors. Therefore, much of the material that was eventually found during agricultural activity or spontaneously unearthed by heavy rain waters was buried again in big trenches instead of being destroyed. Yet, because the rain is so constant and heavy in the Amazon region, eventually relics like the Tapajoara icon were brought back into the light once again.

This statuette was rescued by Barata,[1] who was allowed to dig in a blacksmith's backyard at the Rui Barbosa Ave., Santarém. It was found in a shallow pit among many other "sacrilegious" ceramic objects that had been thrown there by the people who had found them. Unfortunately, no scientific information on the archeological site or stratigraphic studies are available.

Another reason it is difficult to understand this statuette and other material like it is that there is almost no knowledge available about the life of the Tapajó Indians, who were considered extinct by the end of the eighteenth century CE. Very little was written about their culture, legends, or lifestyle. Together with the Marajoara clay work, which comes from an island about 500 kilometers northeast to Santarém, the Tapajoara ceramic is the most elaborate artwork from the pre-colonial time in Brazil.

While we may have more information about the people who inhabited Marajó Island, their artwork differs from the Tapajó area in many aspects. Therefore, it is difficult to understand the latter based on the former, even though we might attempt to find some parallels. Hence, the study of this statuette requires us to compare and contrast its motifs with similar features observed in other cultures, and then further amplify these elements. From a psychological point of view, it is necessary to recall what human beings want to convey whenever they express an image or an idea through an icon.

The universe of icons

The making of statuettes or icons has accompanied human cultural development since time immemorial. We might not be able to affirm what the necessity or impulse was that pulled a human being to make use of clay, stone, or wood in order to fabricate a representation which, in principle, would emulate human form. However, by investigating more deeply the iconographic universe, one cannot help but identify its psychological value as far as the building up of culture is concerned.

Demokritos, a philosopher of Abdera (460 to 370 BCE) spoke of *eidola*, images (sometimes ghosts) that were ceaselessly emitted by objects of all sorts. These *eidola* "carried representations of mental activities, thoughts, characters, emotions of the person/object whom they came. And, thus charged, they have the effect of living agents."[2] Demokritos was one of the first to point out the fact that the unanimated body can make an impression on our psyche as if it were speaking to us.

Jung further subscribed to this idea by saying to his patients that they should keep every piece of artistic material they produced since they are graphic representations of their unconscious processes,

> and by looking at them, these objective forms work back on them [the patients] and they became enchanted. It is to say that the effort to concretize an image offered by the unconscious will have a transformative capacity on the patient's psychology.[3]

In other words, the reason the existence of idols or sacred images can be understood is that "they cast their magic into our system and put us right, provided that we put ourselves into them." Jung goes on to tell us that, "If you put yourself into the icon, the icon will speak to you."

Jung also refers to the statue as both the beginning and the end-product of the alchemical process, the *lapis philosophorum* or its equivalent. In his chapter on Adam and Eve in *Mysterium Coniunctionis*, he utilizes the image of Adam initially as the primordial image to be transformed, and by that he equates it to the beginning of the process.[4] Accordingly, Adam is said to be created as a lifeless statue that undergoes a progressive process of embodiment of divine light, which makes the darkness depart from it, so that love, body, soul, and spirit, all united, become one. And in this, the mystery is hidden. Therefore, after this union, the statue was erected filled with light and divinity.[5]

This is a very encouraging idea because it indicates that the statue "needs" us to become alive. In other words, what we conceive, or what is conceived in us as ideas, requires our aid to become materialized and "functional." In Egyptian and Indian cultures, and in Hebrew and Christian traditions, we can observe the practice of anointing statues as a way to introduce a divine influence or holy emanation, spirit, or power into them. This practice is, in a way, an enactment of the statue's need of a human being's help to become alive.

In Manichaeism, alchemy, and certain Gnostic texts, such as the Mandaean scriptures and fragments, von Franz explains that "the statue has been regarded as a symbol of the resurrected body, and also, as the Second Adam."[6] According to the alchemists:

We die in the first Adam, the corruptible, physical man, while the second Adam, often identified with Christ and sometimes with other savior figures, is the incorruptible Adam and the immortal body. This second Adam is the immortal body which we are supposed to get after resurrection. This second body is like a statue.[7]

In the Manichaean hymns, it is said that towards the end of the world the bad ones will be punished and the good ones will be rewarded when the statue comes.[8] In Greek, the word for "statue" is *andrias*, when it occurs in connection with that idea. It includes *anèr* or "man," which indicates that *andrias* is used only to refer to a stone statue in human shape. Thus, because of the association of the statue with both the redemption and the resurrection, quite often "the later alchemists identified the human-shaped statue with the philosopher's stone, conceiving it the incorruptible part of the personality which survives death."[9] It must be said for the sake of disambiguation that the word "icon," derived from the Greek *eikon*, is sometimes used for "statue," but etymologically this word refers to an image of an effigy used in an abstract sense: "Who is the image [εἰκών – *eikon*] of the invisible God . . ." (Col. 1:15).

Jung also supports the idea that statues are a reservoir of substances from which the process of alchemical transformation can proceed: "That is the statue from whose heart the water is extracted."[10] There was a wide and vast belief that a precious substance was hidden in the statue, and accordingly it was said that "the pagans made statues of Mercurius and hid in them a simulacrum of the god."[11] In this way, they would worship what was really represented inside the image (the essence of the god), and not its externality.[12]

The iconographic images also become a depositary of expectations and propitiations, functioning as intermediaries between human beings and the domain of the gods. In Voodoo practice, for example, images or icons are utilized to emulate certain capacities. They involve magic rituals in which the image is but a substitute for the individual, that is, the graphic representation becomes not only a receptacle for the priest's conjuring, but also as a transmitter of the intentions that have been weaved in order to affect the real human being.

In summary, a human being's relationship to a statue may be considered under the following points:

1   Statues, as *eidola*, may "project" on us whatever their "completion" conveys. They carry a potentiality of their own, which may be transferred to us. This may explain why the adoration of idols or images of saints in the Catholic Church is such an old tradition, and yet is still practiced today. The devotion to the Holy Face of Jesus is a good example of this.

2   When a statue is built out of an inner necessity imposed by the torturing dealings of the unconscious, it may reveal a redemptive prospect. That very image, when freed from the unknowing wrappings of the unconscious, can speak up its own inner truth and make its very meaning recognizable. The Brazen Serpent of Moses has this connotation (Nm. 21:6–9).

3   Statues represent that which will be made alive by means of our own effort.
    For example, Adam, as a statue made out of mud, only started developing
    into an "Anthropos" by the breath of God. Therefore, by modeling a statue
    we are making alive something that is hidden and dormant in ourselves.
4   The statues are the carriers of what we impart on them. They are the guard-
    ians of higher values that we materialize within them. Thus, they represent
    a place where we can come back to objectify our own devotion and faith
    we nurture towards a supernatural reality. The statues lead us to the infinity
    which, in other words, is the way towards the Self.
5   Statues, as *andrias*, are representative of the immortal aspect of ourselves—
    the part that resists death and stands for resurrection.
6   The icons are substitutes for human beings whenever something is supposed
    to be transmitted or transferred to the person.
7   By handling and caring for a statue, be it by means of oiling, washing, offer-
    ing flowers, or lighting candles, we are somehow "recharging" the image
    with its own energy, its Mana, so that it can give us its own energy. It is as if
    by taking care of an image, it ends up taking care of us.

As we attempt to understand the Tapajoara icon, it is helpful to keep in mind the
relationships described above. It is also important to remember that in order to
obtain some sort of knowledge, it is necessary to hold on to a proper attitude. In
the search for the understanding of this image, the discussion of and reflection on
its motifs from the point of view of history, anthropology, and archeology, as well
as mythology, are some of the ways through which we can propitiate the unveiling
of its meaning.

Barata, one of the pioneers of cataloging the Tapajoara ceramic, says that:

> All of the ceramic work of the Tapajó tribe is like that. It speaks! It clarifies as
> if it were a language to which one becomes accustomed and becomes famil-
> iarized with its extremely varied representations. This is the only writing sys-
> tem they left us and, to decipher it, all *conjectures, coming from acceptable
> basis, comparative or deductive, should be allowed* [emphasis mine].[13]

It is quite comforting to know that this gentleman, in the first half of the last
century, paved the road for other disciplines in the quest to understand such material. He collected this icon, classified it, and protected it, before it was kept in the
museum's custody.

Notes

1 Barata, F. (1953). *A arte oleira dos Tapajó. III. Alguns elementos novos para a tipolo-
   gia de Santarém*. Belém: Instituto de antropologia e etnologia do Pará, p. 4.
2 Lindsay, J. (1970). *The origins of alchemy in Graeco-Roman Egypt*. London: Muller,
   p. 95.

3 Jung, C. G. (1976). *Symbolic life*, CW 18, § 413.
4 Jung, C. G. (1970). *Mysterium coniunctionis*, CW 14, § 544 ff.
5 Ibid., § 559.
6 Franz, M. V. (1987). *Individuation in fairytales*. Dallas, TX: Spring Publications, p. 113 ff.
7 Ibid.
8 Ibid.
9 Ibid.
10 Jung, C. G. (1970). *Mysterium coniunctionis*, CW 14, § 560.
11 Ibid., § 564.
12 Lindsay, J. (1970). *The origins of alchemy in Graeco-Roman Egypt*. London: Muller, p. 227 ff.
13 Barata, F. (1950). *A arte oleira dos Tapajó, I: considerações sobre a cerâmica e dois tipos de vasos característicos*. Belém: Instituto de Antropologia e Etnologia do Pará, p. 18.

Chapter 5

The Tapajoara statuette

As we learn from Jungian psychology, the attempt to understand images primarily depends upon the kind of psychic disposition of each individual. There are people who may be captivated by a given image much more by its communal outlook or objective features (extroverted attitude). Others, though, may become fascinated by the image based on their own previous internal experiences (introverted attitude). Regardless of the psychic propensities in the way the individual relates to an image, the process of becoming conscious of it is supported by the four pillars that Jung denominated as functions of consciousness: thinking, feeling, sensation, and intuition. Such functions, in accordance with the attitudinal disposition (extroverted or introverted), work like instruments through which the different aspects amalgamated in a given content can be deciphered. Through this decoding, the ego is capable of making use of its discriminating capacity in order to name, recognize, and judge what has been apprehended.

Considering that the Tapajoara statuette is an obscure object—an orphan of history, context, and proper cultural identification—any objective form of knowledge obtainable from it is prone to bias. Therefore, the symbolic understanding of this icon should not preclude the analyst's methodology that is utilized when working with any material genuinely offered by the unconscious. As mentioned earlier, this statuette entered the analytical setting as if it were a dream, not only because of its numinosity and aesthetics, but also because it was something completely unknown and without context. In this sense, the image should be taken as a product offered by the unconscious.

Nevertheless, the subjective understanding of any material bears with it an experience of incompleteness because the assembling of the symbolic parcels of a given psychic image will inexorably constellate its counterpart. Therefore, it is necessary that each one of the functions of consciousness be summoned during the process so that the image can be objectified to the ego as close as possible to its original meaning.[1] Even though we may never get to the real nature of a given image, it is necessary that we strive to avoid speculation and fantasies about it. First, the image should be considered as objectively as possible, and only afterwards its subjective meaning appreciated. As a matter of fact, the circumambulation of any pictographic material with the four functions of consciousness is another Jungian technique utilized in interpreting dreams and also in extracting consciousness from images that are made available to us.[2]

In the report presented below, we can see that the anthropological information of the statuette (Figures 5.1 and 5.2) was primarily provided by sensory stimulation (sensation function), although we can also see some inferences on given aspects related to the icon (thinking function):

> Anthropomorphic statuette, produced by the Tapajonic[3] pottery (between 900 to 1400 CE), depicting a sitting feminine figure, taking her left foot to her mouth. It has a naturalistic and well proportioned form. Its face presents: eyes, eyebrows, nose and ears; the body shows the breasts, navel, genitals and buttocks. The object is wholly covered with white painting, with straight black lines forming geometrical details on the face, arms and legs. Pulses, ankles and below the knees are embellished made with incisions painted red, probably representing strips of cotton or another fiber. The hair is long and combed into plaits, ornamented with a band made with modeling, incisions and red painting. The body ornamentation indicates a social identity of the individual and suggests a sign of the existence of a group of people who had a differentiated status among the Tapajó people.[4]

In this report, the utilization of the feeling function was practically restricted to the observation that the piece has a "quite naturalistic and well proportioned" form, as if it were a compliment. One of the main attributes of the feeling function is to help us to identify where or in which aspect of the work the energy is concentrated or lacking. In this way, the feeling function is more concerned with value. Based on that, the region of the head is disproportionally bigger than the rest of the body, which suggests that the author/artist was very concerned about this body segment. This supposition is further supported by the fact that there is an elaborate representation of the ornaments present on the head, with special care for the hair. The statuette's sexual characteristics seem, though, to be less emphasized. The breasts are small; only after a closer look at the piece can we identify the gender as female. Continuing with the feeling function, what may be still more relevant is the fact that the statuette was modeled in a peculiar and unusual posture, which is difficult to hold. That is, the figure is sitting up straight and bringing the left foot to the mouth. The image also gives the impression of a serene face, with a distant and indistinct gaze, although the body posture demonstrates perfect balance and flexibility.

If we use the intuition function, this image might refer us back to either an infantile figure or to an adult figure capable of extreme body control. Would this

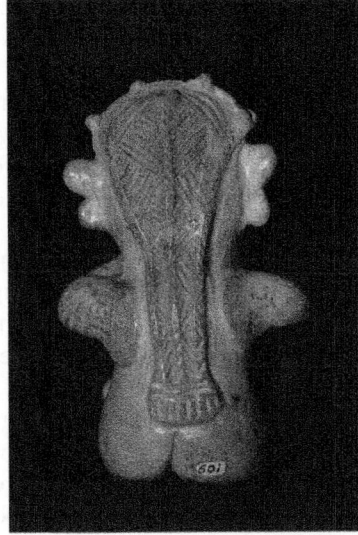

Figures 5.1 and 5.2 Tapajoara anthropomorphic statuette, 900–1400 CE (Emilio Goeldi Museum, Pará).

image be just a toy made by a caring mother or father, a representation of a deity, or the molding of a distinct societal personality belonging to the Tapajó community? In any event, this image is charged with great energy. It has incalculable value because it is the remnant of one aspect of what we, as Brazilians, once were. It also carries something which imparts contemporary psychic equipment, not yet understood, that leaves us with a deep reverential feeling.

Upon this brief and somehow pedagogic circumambulation with the four functions of consciousness, the next step is to compare this statuette with other material in order to amplify some of the identified details that were suggested; therefore, we will move forward in the attempt to come closer to the universe surrounding this statuette.

The statuette and the Beyond

If we look closer at the statuette, we can see an outline around the left eye which alludes to the figure of a scorpion. Some vestiges of paint around the right eye suggest the same design. It has been demonstrated that the contour of the eyes with the form of a scorpion is quite common in the urns of Marajoara pottery

(Figure 5.3); it is associated with the feminine figure and, consequently, with the rites of death.[5] It is possible that this design, both in the urns and on the statuette, could signal a supra-human capacity of glimpsing into other dimensions, or a capacity of seeing things in the dark world.

In the Gilgamesh story, the Scorpion Men guard the mountains through which the Hero needs to go in his quest for the everlasting source of life. This was a realm of complete darkness: "In it there is no light, but the heart is oppressed with darkness. From the rising of the sun to the setting of the sun there is no light."[6] In this Babylonian myth, scorpions have a function of guardians of the threshold of the Beyond since they mediate on what is coming from the world of light and what is not capable of being seen in the dark world.

In the Mithraic cult, Cautopates, one of the two *dadophorae*, is standing besides Mithra during the bull sacrifice. He bears a torch pointing down, which is an allusion to death and to the dying sun, enacted in this sacrificial act. In other representations, Cautopates is depicted holding a scorpion instead of a

Figure 5.3 Funerary urn with scorpionic eyes (Pacoval, in Amapá, northern Brazil).

Figure 5.4 Serket.

torch, which refers to the lack of intensity in solar light that—upon crossing the sign of Scorpio—announces winter in the Northern Hemisphere. The scorpion, as an equinoctial symbol, strengthens the connection between itself and the eternal cycles of death and birth.[7]

In ancient Egypt, at least three feminine deities are associated with scorpions: Serket (Figure 5.4), Ta-Bitjet, and Selkis. Serket is one of the protective deities who guards over the coffins, chests, and jars where embalmed material is kept. Represented in anthropomorphic form with a scorpion on her head, Serket is also associated with the protection of maternity.

Ta-Bitjet is a spouse of Horus, and it is said that the blood that flows after the rupture of her hymen is a panacea against all poisons. Selkis is mentioned as a major figure of the seventh hour in the Amduat (a book on the search for immortality).[8] Her job is to neutralize the action of the serpent Apopis, an enemy who threatens the Pharaoh's resurrection. This terrifying serpent could, with its breath, completely dry up the river where the boat of the Sun-God was sailing. Selkis, then, as a scorpion goddess, has the ability to cut the serpent in several pieces, thus putting it out of action. Possibly, the presence of a scorpion goddess in order to annihilate the serpent is due to the fact that both are venomous creatures, and so the poison of the goddess can neutralize the venom of the snake (*similia similibus curantur*).

This paradoxical aspect of the scorpion is taken up by Jung in his studies on alchemy, where he spoke about the dual aspect of the divine water. He emphasized the creative power of birth and death that it engenders. In this process, he emulated the figure of the Uroborus, since it is the image *par excellence* of self-renewal, as the dragon biting its own tail "slays itself, weds itself and impregnates itself." It is called the living Mercurius, which, in turn, is called "the scorpion, that is, venom: for it slays and brings itself back to life."[9]

In the Maya culture, there is a goddess in the form of a scorpion (Figure 5.5) that holds many of the characteristics of Serket:

> This Scorpion-Mother dwells at the end of the Milky Way, where she receives the souls of the dead; it is through her, being represented as a mother with various breasts where the infants are nurtured, that the souls of the newly-born appear.[10]

In medieval astrology, the sign of Scorpio was associated with the region of the groin and, consequently, to the reproductive area.[11] Von Franz mentions that the words "*stirb*" and "*werde*" ("die" and "born again") are ascribed to this sign, implying a total annihilation and resurrection.[12] The scorpion is thus related to death, resurrection, and maternity in different cultures; in the Hellenic culture, it was also associated with the Great Goddesses.

Another important feature of the scorpion is its capacity to adapt to different surroundings and to survive the most difficult situations. This aspect of roughness and resistance may be a metaphor for the hardships of the path the soul has to take. So, it is possible that the scorpionic design around the eyes of the Tapajora statuette alludes to the matters of the Beyond, for this seems to be an important aspect of the lives of these Indians.

Figure 5.5 Maya scorpion goddess.

From the reports obtained by the chroniclers who navigated the Amazon and its tributaries after the arrival of the Europeans, we can perceive that the Tapajó were seriously concerned about death. It was reported that they would keep the dried-out bodies of their ancestors as mummies. Bettendorf tells of a highly venerated body that was thought of as their *Monhangarypy*, meaning "original" or "creator" (Bettendorff translates it as "first father"), which the Tapajó honored with dances and offerings.[13] It was placed in a chest under the peak of the roof of a house.

In 1682 CE, Father João Daniel described a Tapajó hut in the middle of the jungle with seven mummies. With great mystery, the Indians would adorn the mummies in new clothing on a given day of the year. In this same hut they kept stones destined to be used during the rituals. Each one of these stones had a name and had a specific role in the adoration ritual. There were stones which would preside over weddings, for example, and others to which the Tapajó appealed for successful childbirth, and so on. Missionaries, however, destroyed the mummies and threw the stone idols into the river. We might wonder how much of the Tapajoara culture had been already destroyed by the time Father João Daniel was writing his descriptions, especially if we consider that over 150 years had already passed since these people were first contacted by the Europeans.

Besides mummification and adoration rituals, the Tapajó had other peculiar ways of dealing with their deceased ones, such as endocannibalism (consuming the ground bones of the dead), which was a practice quite common among some South American tribes:

> When dead, the Tapajó kept the bodies inside an ossuary and, when the flesh was already completely dried up, they pulverized the bones and mixed this powder in a drink prepared by them, and drank it. They did that to 'keep their dead inside their bellies, close to themselves.' Without that they thought they would not win wars.[14]

The Tapajó would also enclose a cadaver on a hammock with all the dead one's belongings placed by his or her feet. Additionally, they would set an icon by the deceased's head, which represented some god, and leave the body in a house built for this purpose until full decomposition took place. The bones would be either put in a funerary urn and buried, or ground up and imbibed in an act of endocannibalism.

Endocannibalism has been noted historically, whereas burial practices are noted as an archeological finding. Both practices reveal that the Tapajó dealt with their deceased ones in different ways, suggesting a social hierarchy that includes nobility.

In the early seventeenth century CE, Acuña observed that the Tapajó had distinct ways of handling the dead: "Some were kept inside their own houses, others were burnt in huge bonfires along with all their belongings."[15] It was also reported that the bones of shamans were kept hanging from the hammocks inside their huts, and were adored as ancestor gods.

However, we also need to consider that this information, obtained from several sources at distinct moments and by different individuals, does not allow us to make a concise judgment on how truly the Tapajó conceived death. It is possible that they could really have had distinct ways of dealing with this aspect of life. We might also take into account that some changes occurred over time, maybe even faster than imagined, especially given the constant influence from other tribes, and, more devastatingly, from the colonizers. It is also possible that the reports available to us today might not refer exclusively to the Tapajó, when we bear in mind the early chroniclers' lack of knowledge, scientific rigor, and acquaintance with the "primitive" life. But while I was writing about the Tapajó burial, I had a dream in which a voice whispered in my ear:

> By understanding the level of sophistication a group of people spends with an exequy ritual, one may have a glimpse into how developed this group may be in relation to their conception of their psyche.

This dream suggested that I look further into the motifs I had already analyzed because they could provide me with more information about the Tapajós' lives. I learned that anthropologists and archeologists consider a group of people as having a culture when signs can be identified of the group taking care of their deceased ones by providing some form of burial. Thus, I continued my studies and came to the assumption that, by dealing differently with the corpses, the Tapajó had not only established a hierarchy and nobility, but also conceived the souls, or what is not the physical body, in a different way. Therefore, I realized that the Tapajó may have also had a dual conception of souls as von Franz explains in her book *On Dreams and Death*. She says that people who live close to nature believe that an individual has different souls which separate after death. One of these souls is identified as ego or the free soul. This is the central domain of thinking which may reside in the head, heart, or guts, and survives death to live in the Beyond. This soul would correspond, in Jungian parlance, to the relation between the ego and the Self. Another soul is somehow a minor soul (image soul), which appears in the shadow of a man and is activated in dreams and visions, and in unconsciousness. It may even have an existence outside the individual during one's lifetime as a bush soul or outer soul, or in an object or a container, according to the system of belief. This soul also continues to exist after death, as a ghost.[16]

Even though there might be more than two souls in different cultures, this bipartition is more often seen when different cultures are analyzed. In general terms, there is a kind of soul, more like a spirit, which is free and not necessarily incarnated, while the other is more attached to the body. If we think about this from a depth psychology perspective, it is meaningful because both kinds of souls are part of one psychic totality, the Self. So, the God Image in man possesses one aspect which is not fully incarnated, is purely spiritual, and eternal; and another, demiurgical, which manifests itself in physical matter.[17]

The ancient Egyptians also believed man possessed at least two distinct souls. One, the *Ba* soul, whose form is like a bird or star, moves freely after death, following the bark (boat) of the resurrection procession. The other, the *Ka* soul, is called the vital soul and is confined to the underworld with the corpse. Similarly, the old Chinese view states that upon death, the *Hun* soul separates from the *P'o* soul. The *Hun* is more akin to the spiritual substance, and pertains to the masculine or Yang element, while the *P'o* is more soul-like, feminine, and passive, and thus pertains to the Yin element. The *Hun* soul rises upward, wandering towards the east, while the *P'o* soul sinks down to earth, wandering towards the west.

Both the *Hun* and *Ba* souls strive towards awakening and becoming conscious in order to detach from the "world," as they long for a nearness to God. The *Ka* and *P'o* souls, however, struggle to be reborn in this life or to cause some sort of an effect on their descendants and on the fertility of the earth.[18] The final goal in both ancient traditions is to have these two souls reunited again. By that, life would continue and so the mystery of resurrection would be enacted. According to von Franz, resurrection means, then, the unification of these two aspects of the person; one, like the *Ba* soul, more akin to individuality, and the other, as the *Ka* soul, more related to collectivity.[19]

By envisaging the possibility of resurrection through the reunion of these two souls, something must be done by the individual in his lifetime and by the priests or holy men upon death so that the resurrection may occur. This reunion, then, is to be accomplished for the sake of something which, in psychological language, is more precious than the two alone, that is, the Self. Therefore, it may be inferred that a certain code of ethics and morality must have been established for the group of people who hold the bipartite belief in the souls. Each individual must have had a set of daily "prescriptions" to follow in his or her lifetime in order to propitiate such a reunion. In the Christian belief system, a thorough set of rules is supposed to be observed so that upon the Final Judgment the believer will be reborn in both flesh and soul in everlasting life, as stated in the Credo: *I believe in the resurrection of the flesh and eternal life.*

Thus, when we consider the diversity of indigenous tribes in Brazil, how they spread across the country, and the different sources of information not always collected with scientific methodology, then the study of the conception of "soul" and life after death, especially before colonization, is a rather challenging subject. For example, the Tupinambá Indians believed in a soul with two components, according to Yves d'Évreux, a Capuchin priest who visited the northern Brazilian regions of Maranhão and Pará in the early 1600s CE. For the Tupinambá, the soul that was attached to the body was called *an*, but when it detached from the body it was called *anguere*.[20] This latter soul also meant "everything that heralded an imminent death," which was something that was not quite clear to the Indians, but carried the highest grade of dread.[21] The concept of *anguere* was so frightening, they could faint if they thought that *anguere* was after them.

Thevet, another Catholic priest who visited southeastern Brazil in the late 1500s CE, reported on the belief in life after death among the Tupinambá living in the area. When asked whether the souls survived after the bodies had been destroyed, the chief responded that they would travel to very far places that were rather pleasant and full of joy, where the souls were all gathered together. He also responded that their shamans (*caraíbas*) would visit these souls quite often. It seemed clear that the Indians were terrified when one member of the tribe passed away. They hastened to the funerary ceremonies, and were urged to bring back any belongings that were given by the deceased to someone in the tribe. Nobody dared to keep any of the deceased's belongings, as the tribesmen feared that his *anguere* would come back to retrieve his things, haunt people, and cause disease, and even death.[22]

Not only the Tupinambá, but other Brazilian tribes as the Tembé, Guaraiús, and Apapocuvas-Guarani believed that the

> souls, which are immortals, when detached from the body, were transported to far beyond the mountains (located in the West), where their ancestors lived, if they had proceeded properly in their lifetime. These souls meet there, in this paradise, singing, dancing and having everlasting fun.[23]

According to these reports, the souls of "insignificant or weak (effeminized)" people who could not defend their territory were not allowed to enter the paradise. D'Évreux is not positive whether these Indians believed all women had souls. Women would only get there if they had had a virtuous life, and then, they should be buried alongside the great men, that is, the warriors who had killed and devoured many enemies.[24]

There is no clear information that the Tapajó had a belief system of life after death, and much less that they had different souls. However, it might be possible that they not only had a belief that life would continue after the physical body stopped functioning, but also that there was a kind of afterlife that needed to be cared for. This hypothesis is substantiated by the way they handled their dead, the comparative material presented and amplified earlier in this section, and the following analysis of the motifs associated to the Tapajoara statuette.

The presence of scorpions around the eyes of this statuette and also in other mortuary urns of neighboring Indians, and the ritual of drinking a liquid mixed with ground bone, suggest that the Tapajó had distinct ways of conceiving death. In other cultures, the scorpion, as discussed earlier, points to a conception of something belonging to the individual that will not die but needs to continue through a journey across a dark path. The scorpion would then represent a helping animal during this journey.

The "travel" that is supposed to be undertaken by the soul of the deceased might be further substantiated by the fact that all things belonging to the dead person, including his weaponry, were buried with him. According to D'Évreux, the Tupinambá Indians in the neighboring region of Maranhão were also concerned about the need to keep tending a fire so that the soul would not get lost on its journey to the Beyond. However, when we consider the ritual of drinking the bones, it seems that a second conception about death also exists. Symbolically, bones are that part of the individual that does not die. Dreams of bones frequently stand for that which is kept "alive" from the individual. It is one's essence. So, by drinking what is imperishable, the Tapajó are signaling a belief of something that stays "here," close to them, which must be taken in and re-integrated, so that it will not be left out or lost.

More historical, anthropological, and material evidence is needed for this idea to be confirmed, but it is not an implausible hypothesis. Perhaps the Tapajó dealt with death by keeping in mind two souls: one that travels through a dark path towards redemption, resurrection, or some other ending, and another that does not leave the bones, waiting to be resurrected in the bodies of the living. In any event, we might also infer that the Self, or the idea of something imperishable that needs to be further incarnated, was present among them.

The statuette's religious body

The statuette is shaped in a way so that the figure can remain sitting while resting on a surface. In spite of the weird position of bending one leg to bring the toe to the mouth, there seems to be no difficulty in this movement. The spine is erect, although the same movement in a human being would mean forcing one's head and trunk forward with a necessary twist of the spine. And yet, this is not the case with the figure. Instead, it has a placid countenance that is in deep harmony with its body, and no sign of physical effort is suggested.

Oddness and contorted postures are features mostly found among the Hindu iconographic material and more archaic cultures "that developed bodily techniques for meditation and communication with the supernatural world. When they sat on given postures, they acquired a state of intense concentration which allowed them to evoke cosmological concepts."[25]

The representation of gods and goddesses in postures that are biomechanically difficult to sustain is in deep contrast with the hagiographic material in Christianity. Symbolically, the bodily distortion that is observed with these sacred statues may suggest that the whole being takes part in the process of attaining higher consciousness or redemption. The body (or the instincts) must be considered in the process; they cannot be overlooked; they should also be a coadjutant in the course of communion between humankind and the divine. This participation may be either as a vehicle or as a path through which one achieves deeper knowledge. It is not saying, necessarily, that the body/instinct is fully taken into the process of acquisition of higher consciousness as a raw substance. It is also quite often reshaped (distorted) instead so that body/instinct, in its full energy, can be taken in during the initiatory path.

Physical illness, accidents, and temporary or even permanent disability can be ways the unconscious communicates to an individual that there is a need to change one's life, ways of perceiving the world, relationships with others, or relationship with oneself. The body, thus, can be viewed as both the vehicle and the path in the process of refurbishing oneself. For example, St. Thomas incarnated the need to have an objective sensorial experience to certify the eternal presence of Christ. By touching Christ's wound, he objectively experienced the divinity. In certain ways, many among us still need the wound in the body to be touched by the divine aspects of some of our ordeals in life.

In Christianity, however, things are not so simple. We can see that the images in Catholic iconography are often well-dressed, well-shaped, and well-behaved, and inspire good and pious behavior. Such features reflect that both the body and instinct must be silenced. The body is often depicted imprisoned and the instinct becomes the prey of domestication and repression. One could say that the *matter* that along with the spirit makes up a Christian must be defeated and deprived of any pleasure, as seen in the rituals of auto-flagellation, abstinence, or even fasting. In psychological terms, though, the need to control body/instinct as seen in Christian cults actually ratifies more than assuages their importance for the individual in the process of reaching higher levels of consciousness. That is, even tamed, the body is still a numen, as can be deduced from the Christian hornbook.

The posture observed with the Tapajoara statuette suggests that the body was not overlooked in that society. The statue is naked, so there is no indication that what belongs to the natural human must be hidden. This is true, considering that indigenous cultures still walk freely naked in their territories today. Their bodies are a place for aesthetic and ritualistic manifestations rather than a condition to be hidden, incarcerated, and depotentialized.

There is a well-marked incision on what might be the navel, although it is placed much higher than expected. The breasts are small, but not flaccid, and can hardly be seen from the front. In spite of the vulva being distinctly marked, it is necessary to look closely at the figure in order to be sure the genitals are there, or else it is not possible to be certain if it is a feminine figure.

The neck is overly wide and the head is disproportionally large for the body (contrary to the anthropologist's statement above). The ears are big and protruding, with markings in the way of earrings. This kind of proportion between head, trunk, and limbs is typically found with babies, since the flow of physical development in humans is cephalocaudal (from the head down) and proximodistal (from the center outward). For instance, after birth, what is closer to an infant's head and the upper trunk has larger dimensions as compared to the limbs and what is located downward. As the development goes on, what is farther from the head and trunk continues to grow and reach the proportions we know in adult life.

From a corporeal point of view, it is not possible to ascertain whether the statuette image represents an adult, teenager, or child. We might think that it is a child based solely on the disproportion of the head and muscle flexibility; however, on the other hand, we might think that it is a teenager or adult because it demonstrates good balance in holding a rather extenuating and difficult posture. In addition, the eyes suggest a state of profound meditation, bringing the figure much closer to a representation of someone who has some degree of mental and physical training; that is, a mature adult being.

Under a more pragmatic view, we should keep in mind that some genetic syndromes might lead to similar phenotypic expression. For instance, Turner syndrome is a genetic abnormality that affects only women, and results in short height, the presence of pterygoid neck ripples (a webbed neck), the absence of or very few pubic hairs, and small breasts. Ears are generally lower on the head, and due to the ripples the neck seems to be thicker than usual. The size of the body is typical, but the limbs are shorter. Generally, there is no intellectual impairment, but the women never menstruate and cannot bear children.

Another genetic disorder, Down's syndrome, often results in loose ligaments, ripples at the neck, and eyes similar to those of Asian people. Hence, we might find that a genetic syndrome among primitive communities could give reason to some kind of worship. As previously mentioned, the occurrence of a physical lesion (genetic, congenital, or acquired) among Mesoamericans was considered a sign of association between a human and the divine, and there were many iconographic images that represented people with such physical deformities.

Nevertheless, even though this statuette may represent someone with a physical impairment due to a genetic dysfunction, the fact that she is in a position with her toe in her mouth is quite peculiar and may have a purpose. Its purposiveness may be further appreciated when we consider it together with the well-cared-for hair, the diadem or crown, the neck covering, the ornaments, and the body paintings. In other words, the posture and the ornaments seem to point to some symbolic form of the feminine figure that is represented in its ritualistic, ceremonial, or mystic character.

When we take these characteristics into account from a comparative point of view, the Tapajoara statuette appears to be the opposite representation of the primitive Great Goddesses where there is clearly an emphasis on the breasts, belly, and buttocks, and the head is proportionally smaller in relation to the body. On the other hand, it is common for feminine deities to be represented sitting on the ground. According to Neumann, "This 'sedentary characteristic,' where the buttocks form the antithesis of the feet, the symbol of freedom of movement, represents a close link with the earth."[26] Ritualistically, sitting upon something means taking possession of it. But, other than the sitting position, this Tapajoara image gives no indication of being a Great Goddess in her reproductive aspect or as an amalgamator of life, taking over the never-ending source of creation, the earth.

It has been reported that the Tapajós' religious life was very intense and the feminine was revered, although there are no specific reports on how it was enacted in practice. Very little is known about these people. They apparently did not speak Tupi, the most prevalent language among the early Brazilians. However, from the limited material that was left by the early chroniclers who had close contact with them, we can see that there are some similarities between the Tupi or Guarani speakers across the country (even across the continent of South America) and the Tapajó. The similarities observed in the culture among the many tribes that inhabited such a vast territory lead us to believe that some practices in religious life and social organizations were also shared between the Tapajó and these other tribes.

According to Couto Magalhães,[27] one of the most prominent Brazilian scholars, who spent most of his lifetime among the Brazilian Indians and wrote Tupi grammar, the idea of an Almighty God was not present among the Brazilian Indians by the time of the "discovery of Brazil." As with the religious system of many archaic cultures in their primordial times of development, there were many deities among the Brazilian indigenous people. Thus, there was no word in the Tupi-Guarani language that could express this idea of a monotheistic entity. However, a superior principle named Tupã was considered as having precedence over all the others.

It is interesting to note that one idea was prevalent among these Brazilian Indians: All created things have a mother. The word "father" was not used. In fact, *father* only began to be associated with the origin of humankind where the marriage had already excluded the "community of women," that is, a woman would be linked only to one man and society would be under male dominance. So, the idea was that all created things had a mother, but the word "father" may not have been part of the belief system of the Brazilian Indians who lived in such a rudimentary level of civilization. The Roman aphorism *pater est is quem justae nuptiae demonstrant*[28] explains the idea that, in primitive societies, it was the word "mother" that was utilized to determine filiation.

The same idea of the all-pervading motherhood can also be appraised in the Judeo-Christian tradition, for, according to the Bible, "Adam called his wife's name Eve; because she was the mother of all living" (Gen. 3:20). The word *"Eve"* in Hebrew comes from ḥawwâ, which means "living" or "life."

So, in a certain way, among the Tupi or Guarani speakers, the feminine had a prominent role in the society. As mentioned earlier, even though the Tapajó did not speak the Tupi language (which has still not been proven), it is not impossible that they shared many religious aspects common to other tribes. The idea that the feminine had a remarkable importance among these early settlers of the Pindorama[29] can be further appreciated in the Tupi theogony.

Magalhães tells us that there were three superior gods: the Sun, who is the creator of all living things (fauna); the Moon, who creates the flora; and Perudá or Rudá, the god of love (more like Eros), whose task is to promote reproduction among the living created beings.[30] Each one of these three gods was aided by other gods whose number was equal to the genera of living beings recognized by the Indians, that is, each living being within the fauna, the flora, or the mineral domain. These latter gods, in turn, were further helped by as many other entities as the number of known species. Therefore, each lake, river, plant, and animal had its own protector genie; actually, "its mother." Among the Indians of Mato Grosso and Goiás (in the central part of Brazil), especially the Pará Indians and probably the Amazonas, this was still true by the turn of the nineteenth century CE, and even today.

These gods did not have abstract qualities that characterized supernatural features. Therefore, there were no abstract terms to indicate them. They were only referred to as "mother of the living," "mother of the vegetation," and so on. The word for "Sun" in Tupi is *Guaracy* (or *Coaraci*), from *Guara* ("living being" or "luminous"), and *Cy* ("mother"). The Tupi word for "Moon" is *Jacy*, from *Ja* ("vegetation") and *Cy* ("mother"). There are reports that the Tapajó worshiped the Moon, and that the New Moon was especially honored.[31] When She appeared it was time for the mothers to bring their children to be blessed by the Moon in a ritual involving dance, joy, and faith.

These Tupi and Guarani Indians had a large number of idols but it seems that the female ones were predominant since they were supposed to protect different aspects of daily life. They were all known as "Mothers" in relation to the Tupi-Guarani speakers. Some of these include the Mother of Labor/Pregnancy (Mambixemã-Manha), the Mother of Love (Taicuçá-Manha), the Mother of Fishing (Pira-Ci), the Mother of Rice (Aruatila), the Mother of Manioc (Maniocki), the Mother of Corn (Aruati-Ci), and the Mother of Woods (Caã-Manha).[32] There were also iconographic representations of "Fathers," but they were much smaller in number. The question of whether or not this Tapajoara statuette is another of these "Mother" figures is left open to discussion. But we must ask ourselves: What would she have mothered?

The idea that the Tapajó may have spoken a very specific dialect (not Tupi or Guarani) is supported by the information that the Jesuits, when they came to these people, had to prepare a new translation of the Bible because "they didn't speak the Common Language,"[33] that is, Tupi. Tupi-Guarani, however, is a rather large linguistic trunk that has more than one hundred different languages derived from it. Among this hundred, there are many more dialects, which may cause misunderstanding even among groups of people who could have been somehow related genetically, ethnically, geographically, or linguistically. Therefore, when we attempt to draw conclusions about the Tapajó culture based exclusively on the comparative material gathered from other tribes, we must proceed with caution.

When the scarce information gathered from the earlier chroniclers about the Tapajó is contrasted with the mythological or religious material from other distant Brazilian tribes, such as the ones located in distant regions of Mato Grosso by the border of Paraguay and Bolivia, we can see that there are many similarities to consider when we seek to understand this culture. Bettendorf, for example, reported that one of the main "deities" among the Tapajó was a White Deer with fiery eyes. This same motif is spread throughout the country and, in Tupi-Guarani lexicon, the white deer is more often called *Anhangá*, and is usually a doe.[34]

Looking at the bodily characteristics present in the statuette, we can see that a red structure covers the head. It has a form of either a crown or diadem with four projections. The hair, neatly arranged in plaits on the back of the head, reaches down close to the waistline, and seems to be covered with what appears to be a veil. However, we cannot assume that it is a veil, but rather a "nape cover," which has been commonly observed in other clay anthropomorphic figures from Santarém. The nape cover represents people of a certain social position or even shamans.

The four projections crowning the diadem are reminders of the idea of totality engendered by the number 4. In different parts of their work, Jung and von Franz have both pointed out that the quaternary representations are commonly associated with unification, the end of a cycle, and an attempt to reach a more well-balanced psychic condition.

Among the still-existent statuettes from the Tapajó tribe, many are represented wearing a diadem with three or four projections, independent of gender. We can find statuettes of female and male shamans or people of high rank wearing this kind of adornment. So, the number of projections may have a specific meaning that is not yet understood. Travelers who visited the Tapajó between the sixteenth and seventeenth centuries CE reported that men would come to noble women for counseling and oracle consultation.[35] Thus, in a way, it could be concluded that women had a special responsibility or duty among these people, and that the number of projections references the rank or function of the people who wore them.

From all we have analyzed about the Tapajó, it appears that the feminine was worshiped and respected among them. Some scholars even conjecture that the Tapajó could have had a matriarchal society. Bettendorf reported the existence of a "Princess" called Maria Moaçara. She was only "married to someone of equal nobility" and her name, Moaçara, means "very noble."[36] Indeed, she was married to the chief of the Tapajó or the "Principal Roque." The political role of this female nobility seems to be quite evident when we read Bettendorf's account: "The Indians choose to go, besides to their Principaes (Tapajó leaders), to a woman of higher nobility, for consultation in different matters of life, as an oracle, and they would follow strictly whatever she would vaticinate."[37] When Maria Moaçara passed away, Bettendorf reported that an ex-Jesuit priest, Sebastião Teixeira, married

> an Indian belonging to the blood of the 'principaes,' in the hope that he could inherit the principalship, considering that his wife was the closest relative to the Princess Moaçara. However, the Indians did not take him seriously and 'sent him away to another village, far up alongside the river.'[38]

No final conclusions can be made at the moment regarding the meaning of the form of the statuette. The intention may not have been to portray *ipsis corporis*, an ordinary person from the community, but rather someone of higher social or religious rank. And it cannot be affirmed that such an icon represents a goddess, even though her adornments and tattoos could possibly refer to some sort of mystery ruled by Her. The scorpion tattoos around the eyes and the posture of the foot brought to the mouth recall both death and resurrection, referring us back to the possibility that the Tapajó were concerned about the individual's destiny after death. This outlook might become more substantiated as we examine the motif of feet in the coming section.

Notes

1 For a better understanding of attitude and functions of consciousness, see *Psychological Types*, CW 6.
2 Abt, T. (2006). *Introduction to picture interpretation according to C. G. Jung.* Einsiedeln: Daimon, p. 46.
3 The author utilizes the word "Tapajonic" instead of "Tapajoara."
4 Personal information provided by the anthropologist Vera Guapindaia for this book.
5 Schaan, D. P. (1997). *A linguagem iconográfica da cerâmica Marajoara: Um estudo da arte pré-histórica na Ilha de Marajó, Brasil, 400–1300AD.* Porto Alegre: EDIPUCRS, p. 118.
6 Kovacs, M. G. (2004). *The epic of Gilgamesh.* Stanford, CA: Stanford University Press, p. 76.
7 Jung, C. G. (1979). *Symbols of transformation*, CW 5, § 294.
8 Abt, T., & Hornung, E. (2003). *Knowledge for the afterlife: the Egyptian Amduat – a quest for immortality.* Zurich: Living Human Heritage Publications, p. 90.
9 Jung, C. G. (1970). *Mysterium coniunctionis*, CW 14, § 105.
10 Santillana, G. D., & Dechend, H. V. (2007). *Hamlet's mill: an essay on myth and the frame of time.* Boston: David R. Godine, p. 295.
11 von Franz, M. (1998). *On dreams and death: a Jungerian interpretation.* Chicago, IL: Open Court, p. 98.
12 von Franz, M. (1987). *Individuation in fairytales.* Dallas, TX: Spring Publications, p. 86.
13 Bettendorff, J. F. (2010). *Crônica da missão dos padres da Companhia de Jesus no Estado do Maranhão.* Brasília: Senado Federal, p. 354.
14 Guapindaia, V. L. (1993). *Fontes históricas e arqueológicas sobre os Tapajó: A coleção Frederico Barata do Museu Paraense Emílio Goeldi.* São Paulo: anexo 1, p. 14.
15 Acuña, C., Esteves, A. R., Milton, H. C., & Juez, A. S. (1941). *Novo descobrimento do rio Amazonas.* Brasiliana 2, vol. 203. São Paulo: Cia. Ed. Nacional, p. 201.
16 von Franz, *On dreams and death: a Jungian interpretation*, p. 115.
17 Ibid. p. 115.
18 Ibid., p. 116.
19 Ibid., p. 115.
20 D'Évreux, Y., Denis, F., Marques, C. A., & Duarte, S. M. (2002). *Viagem ao norte do Brasil: Feita nos anos de 1613 a 1614.* São Paulo: Editora Siciliano, p. 110.
21 Métraux, A. (1979). *A Religião dos Tupinambás* (Brasiliana 267). São Paulo: Cia. Editora Nacional, p. 56.
22 Ibid., p. 56.
23 Ibid., p. 111.
24 D'Évreux, Y., Denis, F., Marques, C. A., & Duarte, S. M. (2002). *Viagem ao norte do Brasil: Feita nos anos de 1613 a 1614.* São Paulo: Editora Siciliano, p. 297.
25 Words used to describe an anthropomorphic collection at the Gold Museum in Bogota, Columbia.
26 Neumann, E. (1963). *The Great Mother: an analysis of the archetype.* New York, NY: Bollingen Foundation, p. 98.
27 Magalhães, G. C., Magalhães, D. C., & Moreira, V. (1975). *O selvagem: Ed. comemorativa do centenário da 1a ed.* Belo Horizonte: Ed. Itatiaia, p. 81.
28 Father is whom the matrimony indicates.

29 This is the Tupi-Guarani name of Brazil. It means the "region or land of the palm-tree."

30 Magalhães, G. C., Magalhães, D. C., & Moreira, V. (1975). *O selvagem: Ed. comemorativa do centenário da 1a ed.* Belo Horizonte: Ed. Itatiaia, p. 82.

31 Amorim, A. T. (2000). *Santarém: Uma síntese histórica.* Canoas, RS: Editora da ULBRA, p. 26.

32 Ibid., p. 27.

33 Guapindaia, V. L. (1993). *Fontes históricas e arqueológicas sobre os Tapajó: A coleção Frederico Barata do Museu Paraense Emílio Goeldi.* São Paulo: p. 28.

34 Magalhães, G. C., Magalhães, D. C., & Moreira, V. (1975). *O selvagem: Ed. comemorativa do centenário da 1a ed.* Belo Horizonte: Ed. Itatiaia, p. 84.

35 Guapindaia, V. L. (1993). *Fontes históricas e arqueológicas sobre os Tapajó: A coleção Frederico Barata do Museu Paraense Emílio Goeldi.* São Paulo: p. 11.

36 Bettendorf, J. F. (1909). Chronica da Missão dos Padres da Companhia de Jesus no Estado do Maranhão. In: *Revista do Instituto Histórico e Geográfico Brasileiro.* Tomo LXXII. Parte I. Rio de Janeiro: p. 172.

37 Ibid.

38 Ibid.

Chapter 6

The statuette's foot

The most striking characteristic of the Tapajó statuette is that the left foot is brought to the mouth, insinuating that the big toe is being sucked. This particular gesture is peculiar in Brazilian iconographic material as well as other cultures around the world; therefore, it is necessary to investigate this theme more broadly, so that we might appreciate its meaning.

A naïve and puerile form is most commonly observed when a child sucks its own toe. The first impression is that the baby is calm and finds great pleasure in the foot for it soothes the suckling reflex. Generally, this habit occurs when the baby is around five or six months old and can roll over and is ready to start sitting up. It is a pleasant sight for almost anyone to watch a little child doing this as it represents a moment when the child is usually self-centered.

This posture also implies that the child is trying to centralize something; what is more distant from the baby is brought back to the highest center of energy of the body, that is, the mouth. From a neurological standpoint, the baby is reaching forward, getting to know how far it can spread out in the world—a way of knowing itself. The mouth, for an infant at this age, can be considered the vital structure, the axis through which the child's entire development depends. Therefore, what is fundamental for the baby comes to its mouth. Through this gesture the baby proceeds to build up its body image, a milestone that occurs around two months of age. Symbolically, this is an act which allows the baby to incorporate what is farther away from itself, but still touchable. Therefore, it is an act of integrating parts of the outer world.

The act of sucking fingers or toes is a normal occurrence in a child's development, especially because the sucking reflex is fully charged in this stage of life. As an instinct, it requires prompt satiation. But whenever this reflex persists beyond the time of development and acquires pathological significance, it must be analyzed as a symptom. Even though this symptom might be caused by a variety of pathological conditions, psychologically it stands for the absence of symbolic nurturing.

In this context, the emphasis is in what is lacking instead of what is needed. The fixation on this kind of behavior is not uncommon among children who have autism or children whose homes cannot afford adequate psychic support.

Therefore, whenever a child sucks a finger or toe beyond the expected time, it may imply that it is searching in itself for a kind of psychic "food" or nourishment it cannot find in its surroundings.

Images of the foot brought to the mouth can also be seen in different cultures, within different contexts. It is quite common for Krishna, for example, to be represented lying down, sucking his foot smeared with butter as a result of his mischief. He is worshipped among the Hindus as an avatar of Vishnu, and his popularity comes from the humanized form that is referred to in the Hindu epic stories. His deeds, known as Krishna Leela, contain popular themes, and he is frequently depicted as a rather developed mischievous child who steals butter.

There is a Hindu myth about a wise man called Markandeya, who describes a vision he had of Krishna (or Vishnu) in the form of a baby sucking his right toe, lying on a fig leaf, while floating on the rough waters of the vast primordial ocean (Figure 6.1). When the wise man asks Lord Krishna the secret behind the apparition, He answers: "I am the Primal Cosmic Man, Narayana. I am Master of

Figure 6.1 Krishna licking his foot (drawing based on a glass painting, Shashwati Women's Museum).

the Waters." Other stories say that Markandeya, when he tries to touch Vishnu's feet, is drawn into His body during His inspiration. From inside Vishnu's body, Markandeya sees the earth, the sky, the stars, the devas, and the demons. He also sees his own group of devotees (his ashram), its forests, and rivers. He then feels Time as if he is passing through the Yugas (Eons) and, suddenly he sees the Pushpa-Bhadra River flowing peacefully beside his ashram.[1]

Another image that depicts the foot brought to the mouth is of the boy called Naranua, a Hindu god of the spirit. He is represented as a handsome boy resting on a coiled-up serpent with his toe in his mouth. The Purana, one of the eighteen sacred texts of the Hindu Vedas, written between 200 BCE and 800 CE, tells us that the River Ganges flows from the toenail of the left foot of Krishna, washing the face of the moon and forming the four rivers of the earth. Krishna, as Vatapatrashayi, is also represented sucking his left toe, while Brahma emerges from his navel as Krishna's own creation (Figure 6.2).

The stomapod image of the child Krishna has other aspects that might still have psychological value. First, it illustrates both the possibility of and the necessity for psychical nurturing an individual should get based upon the bodily structure he or she utilizes to stand up to the world. It is as if we accommodate that part of ourselves which connects us to the earth, in an act of honoring that which sustains us

Figure 6.2 Brahma being created while Vatapatrashayi Krishna sucks his left foot (drawing based on a bronze sculpture from Asian Civilisations Museum).

in the world (our feet), and helps us to prevail over the rough "lands" of existence. The act of self-sucking represents, therefore, the fundamental need human beings have to find the source of nourishment in themselves.

Second, the appearance of Krishna as a child also relates to the fact that the disturbances, which come along with the developmental process, should be faced with a certain amount of ingenuity. In other words, we must allow for an attitude of non-direct confrontation with the major forces of our daily ordeals. Self-sucking could be viewed here as an introjection of libido, so that an inner balance could be reestablished, that is, come back to Tao, as ancient Chinese wisdom instructs.

The third aspect to be considered refers to the notion of omni-chronicity (Latin: *omnus* = all, whole; and *chronos* = time), that is, a time that encompasses everything that was created at given moments during existence. In the Hindu myth, Markandeya experiences time as if he were floating through the Yugas. It indicates that whenever one is in contact with the ordering center of psychic activities—the Self as defined by Jung, or the image of God as defined by religion—human existence comes into relativity, being no more than an instant of the divine act of creation, or, under a mystic view, becomes indissoluble in relation to the divine, thus stepping out of the conception of time.

To experience the Self or to have a mystical experience is to assume a deflation of the ego or even an emptying of the ego (*Kenosis*), which needs to make room for the divine. When the ego deflates or empties, it allows a human being to glimpse eternity. *Kenosis* is, in a way, the act of becoming a child again, as described in Mark 10:15, or being like the child Krishna lying on the fig leaf. Some people have a numinous experience of the Self in the eminence of death and they later describe it as having seen their whole life in a few seconds. Therefore, the image of the stomapod conveys what could become a numinous experience for an individual, because once it suscitates the need to come to terms with our inner source life, we may eventually find the gods, or the Self, which can be something humanely challenging to bear.

The issue of the toes

In the previous chapters, we discussed how different segments of the lower limbs are connected to creativity. However, there is a particular form of creativity that is expressed by the feet and toes, and more specifically by bringing them to the mouth. The creation prompted by this posture appears to be related to the aspect of self-creation. Or, in other words, that which is being created sprang from the agent who fertilizes itself; an offspring results from an act of self-impregnation.

Psychologically, this posture is very instructive once it shows that a human can engender transformation through the act of self-fertilization and self-renewal. This may be the great opus of the analytical work. One of the prerogatives of psychotherapy is to midwife the individual in the process of getting in contact with himself or herself. The deeper analysands can penetrate their own being, the more they impregnate themselves, not only from the Self where they inhabit, but also from the aspect which dwells in the Self. Through that, they may become what they are meant to be. In this way, the individuation process can be understood as self-fertilization.

While taking this idea of creativity or self-fertilization into account, we can see how the participation of the big toe seems to present an archetypal characteristic, especially if we consider the large number of these images that can be found in other cultures. In the I Ching, for example, Hexagram 31 refers to "universal engendering." It can be read in the first line that the manifestation of an idea, the possibility for the realization of something, even before it is actually carried out, is present in the big toe. In the commentary of this hexagram, it states: "The idea of an influence is already present, but it is not immediately apparent to others. As long as the intention has no visible effect, it is of no importance to the outside world."[2] Psychologically speaking, this means that the outer manifestation of a creative act cannot prescind from its previous existence in the generating matrix, that is, the unconscious. And because of that, it is necessary that the locus it latently inhabits be reached, so that the creative act can be channeled and eventually consummated. Therefore, the big toe works as the mediator for that which is potentially realizable.

Among the Pawnees, a Native American tribe from the Midwestern United States, the big toe is allegorically celebrated as another creative bodily segment. During a ceremony, the shaman draws a circle on the ground with his big toe that represents the eagle's nest. It is drawn with the hallux because the eagle builds its nest with its claws. By imitating the eagle, the Pawnees are thinking of Tirawa, who makes the world for the people to live in.[3] In this ceremonial act, we can also see how the toe can serve as the mediator of the Self in its circle/nest allegory.

In Eastern traditions, the big toe appears to represent the locus where the potentiality for the realization of anything contained in the individual is projected. The feet as a whole are also understood as the intermediary element or mediator between the material world and the more subtle levels of existence in mythology and in some mystical traditions. For example, the following Tantric text explains how the big toe (specifically of the left foot) becomes a way to connect with Shiva:

> The totality of the satguru is contained in his feet once all the nervous currents end there. The vital spots in each organ of the inner, astral, and mental bodies and the soul are there. Touching the feet, we touch the spiritual master. The mystics teach us that the big toe of the left foot "exhales" the most blissful grace. According to this tradition, the left big toe is connected to the pituitary gland of the guru, which is the door open to Brahma, right inside the Sahasrara Chakra, where, in contemplation, the guru is united with Shiva.[4]

The text goes on to say that, by touching the sandals of the satguru, it is possible to feel his vibrations, which enables one to contact the physical, astral, and mental bodies as well as the soul of the teacher through his feet. It might be highlighted that the big toe works as a spiracle where, in the human being, the flow of energy between body and earth occurs.

As said previously, in some cultures, high-ranked people such as kings were forbidden to touch the soil directly lest their vital fluid be lost to the ground. But in other belief systems, such as Hinduism, this connection was considered more prospectively. The contact between *padas* ("feet") with *prithvi* ("earth") allowed for telluric energy to flow through the great toe, healing both the body and the mind.

When we consider that the feet incorporate such a catalyzing faculty and are metaphorically generative organs themselves, we can see how they came to represent the projection of sexual images in several cultures around the world. For instance, among the Macurapes, an Indian tribe from the northern part of Brazil (Rondônia) there is a legend which says that, in the beginning, the children were born out of a woman's toenail. This was because the men only had intercourse with women through their toenails since they had no vagina at that time.[5] Among the Yurakaré, another Brazilian tribe living by the Mamoré River (along the border between Brazil and Bolivia), it is said that Karu, a cosmogenic being, made a son out of his toenail.[6]

Another example can be found in *The Worship of Priapus*, a book dated from 1786 CE, where Richard Payne Knight described the practices on behalf of St. Cosme, the protector of virility and fertility. In the text, the phallus is called "The Big Toe."[7] And, among the Bambara people of West Africa, the spot between the big and second toes was sexually significant as they believed it had a nervous center with "strings" to control the muscles of the sexual organs and the anus. The Pygmies of the Congo believed that heroes are born from the big toe instead of the vulva.[8]

In acupuncture and reflexology, there are points in the big toe that stimulate the pituitary and the pineal glands, which "are centers for ecstatic vision and sexual stimulation."[9] The big toe has a remarkable function from a sexual and visionary point of view in both Kabbalistic and Tantric literature. In the Kabbalistic tradition, the foot is viewed as a "euphemism for the phallus, both human and divine," while the toes represent the "ten demonic powers."[10] As a Tantric practice, while the erection of his penis is in process, the Yogi alters his breathing rhythm by massaging the big toe because it possesses a nervous extremity, which regulates all the cyclical changes and rhythms of the whole body.

However, it is worth emphasizing the differences regarding mystic sexuality in the Kabbalah and in Tantrism. In both, the sexual act should be carried out in a sober manner, with a certain mystical conscience that accompanies the physical act, but intercourse as a vehicle for spiritual experience is seen differently. In the Kabbalah, the mystical union of thought with its source is fundamental for attaining its main objective, which is procreation. But in the Tantric system, the mystical conscience, or *bodhicitta*, is an end in itself, and this perfect state is obtained through the immobilization of the semen flow (non-ejaculation). The Kabbalists place mystical union at the service of procreation, whereas Tantrism places sexual intercourse without ejaculation at the service of a mystical conscience.

In his 1810 book *Hindu Pantheon*, Edward Moor reproduced a figure of Narayana with the left big toe in his mouth.[11] This figure is similar to the Krishna images described earlier; however, in this particular image, Narayana is not depicted as a child. Rather, the posture is a yogic technique where, "by putting the toe in the mouth and holding it there, it is possible to stop the flux of psychic air in the body."[12] This technique could facilitate control over the seminal flux during a prolonged erection.

In his book *Why Mrs. Blake Cried*,[13] Schuchard analyzes William Blake's spiritual search through sexuality, in both the teachings of Tantric Yoga and of the Kabbalistic traditions, in order to remedy his conflicts in this area. William Blake seems to have used this gathered knowledge when considering the left foot as "a vehicle for spiritual ascension" in his poem "Milton."[14] In this work, Blake registers his metaphysical concerns between man and God and conjectures on personal, political, and cosmic matters that might be intermingled during the process of building a New Jerusalem "on the pleasant green lands of England."[15] Milton is called up from Paradise to join Blake in this task but it was necessary for Blake to absorb the errors of Milton, that is, misogynic Puritanism, before redeeming him. The mystical union between the spirit of Blake and that of the poet, whom he admired so deeply, occurs at the big toe of Blake's left foot (Figure 6.3).

As in Kabbalistic symbolism, the feet may be considered the connector between the natural man and the natural world. This is a peculiar image, considering that whenever a phenomenon is supposed to be "integrated" it usually makes use of the body's orifices, especially the mouth. The use of the left big toe as a place for spiritual integration between Milton and Blake seems, therefore, to be specific to this yogic/Kabbalistic teaching.

However, the association of the image of the feet with raw sexuality is still so pervasive, even in modern times, that Freud took up the matter of the foot fetish, especially related to masculine psychology. According to Freud, the strong attraction a man feels towards feet is related to the son's refusal to accept the absence of a penis in his mother. Upon confirming the absence and the fear of castration brought by this image, the boy then "engenders" a substitute for the penis, and begins to idolize her feet. This worship then would apparently bring back his mother's penis in his psyche. In other words, according to Freud, a man's fetish for feet is due to a distorted view of a missing penis in a woman.

A more extreme kind of feet fetishism can be seen in the Chinese culture. Before Mao abolished foot binding in 1949, it was a common practice to wrap women's feet to prevent them from growing naturally. This cultural tradition was desirable for aesthetic reasons among women and strongly encouraged by men. One of the reasons for this custom is related to Empress Taki (twelfth century CE) who, reportedly, was born with malformed feet (*talipes*) and had to wrap them with bandages. Her female subjects then began to wrap their own feet to be more like her. Men then encouraged the habit because, besides its aesthetic appeal, foot binding also reinforced their male authority—a woman with deformed feet has less probability of fleeing from her husband. Gangrene soon

Figure 6.3 Mystical union between the spirit of Milton and William Blake through the latter's left foot (drawing based on Blake's illustration, the William Blake Archive).

became commonplace, and often the limb had to be amputated. In this example, it is easy to see how the Chinese culture strongly favors the masculine. Even today in China, unfortunately, girls make up the greater number of children in orphanages and a son is the common preference.

The Chinese cultural tradition of wrapping and mutilating the feet might symbolize the lack of understanding of the feminine contents (anima) in the psyche of the Chinese man, as well as the state of awe and terror she may give rise to. Generally, one might conclude that a Chinese man is capable of having an erotic relationship with the feminine only if he can rule over it and shape it to the size of his own psychology. On the other hand, the Chinese woman, with her consent, continues to perpetuate the tradition, perhaps because of a strong positive paternal complex or a rather destructive animus who prevents her from walking with her own legs or, in this case, with her own feet.

Even when a sexual act is considered, the analysis of the images of Shiva as a child and as an adult, as well as the discussion of the foot/toe in mystical traditions, both illustrate that a higher form of creativity is at work. With Blake, these body segments were more explicitly connected to a form of distinct spiritual integration. With the Tapajoara statuette, though, one may not talk about sexuality in its biological aspect per se, from what is depicted in the statuette. Instead, we must keep the phallic aspect of the statuette in mind, in the basic sense, which is "the source of life and libido, the great creator and worker of miracles."[16] We do not have any other material for comparison; therefore, it is legitimate to argue, based on what has been discussed about the symbolism of the foot/toe, that this image might prompt something of a higher order of creation.

The big toe, being the end part, or alternatively the initial part of the human being, seems to serve as a spiracle through which the flow of energies between the outer world and the body is established. And so, if we maintain the suggestion that the feet are the most favorable place for the transit of the vital energies between the individual and the telluric or cosmic universe, then what might be the meaning of an individual constantly feeding from himself?

The statuette and the Uroborus

If we continue supporting the assumption that the feet are one of the preferable loci wherein the exchange of creative flow between man and universe occurs, both in its telluric or cosmic aspects, what could be thought of these body segments when it appears that the individual is nurturing out of them? Usually, images that are suggestive of self-feeding and depict the act of biting a segment of the body, be it the tail, feet, or any other distal part of the body, are commonly associated with the Uroborus. Originally, this expression referred to the figure of the dragon or serpent which bites or suckles its own tail. It is largely present in literature representing, in principle, a symbolic condition where the opposites are united. Etymologically, this word comes from the Greek οὐροβόρος, meaning "to bite its own tail." The Tapajoara statuette was modeled in this way, that is, in the form of bringing the distal part of its foot, the toe, to its mouth. Thus, it is an anthropomorphic representation of the Uroborus figure.

Neumann refers to the Uroborus as an autarchic condition, one where the image presumes a system which is auto-creating, self-sufficient, and independent from the "other." This symbol pervades primitive cultures, and one of its most ancient representations can be found in the jade dragon of the Hongshan culture (China, 4700–2920 BCE), where it is biting its own tail.

From a psychological point of view, depending on how the Uroborus is graphically depicted, it is possible that distinct levels of psychic functioning or stages are being suggested. A zoomorphic Uroborus, for example, where only animal beings are depicted, may suggest that, whatever their contents might mean, they are not close to consciousness. These animal figures are probably more related to the domain of the instincts. This zoomorphic Uroborus could also be pointing to a more archaic psychic development. In this context, the word *archaic* should be taken in a rather broad sense, since it might point to a primitive lifestyle in relation to instinct fulfillment. But it could also point to a higher level of spiritualization. The animals, even living under the domain of the instincts, should be considered the most pious beings because they fulfill their destiny, which makes this paradox tenable. For that matter, Jung considered animals one of the best examples of the individuation process.

The Uroborus translates a primordial condition where there is no differentiation between consciousness and the contents of the unconscious. The Uroboric stage illustrates the psychic condition of the archaic man, who went through life as part of nature and was completely dependent on natural events. Neumann characterizes the Uroborus as the stage of conscious development where the ego is still in an embryonic state and the individual is not distinct from nature, living deeply and syntonically with it, without differentiation.

On the other hand, if this idea of totality is represented by human beings or divine anthropomorphic beings, the Uroborus may indicate an integration of opposites on a higher level.

It is also important to note that other images of the Uroborus contain both anthropomorphic and zoomorphic figures. For instance, Harpokrates (the infantile form of Horus), as a "solar child," is contained in the dragon-shaped Uroborus, sitting on a lotus flower, bringing his thumb to his mouth. The two lions, as guardians of the rising and the setting sun, are called Sef and Tual (Yesterday and Tomorrow) and indicate the child's regenerating feature (Figure 6.4). Harpokrates was conceived by Isis from the lifeless body of Osiris. His name alludes to his weak or deformed legs, and his birth is evidence that Osiris has not perished.

The image of Harpokrates is commonly associated with fragility and frailty. According to Plutarch, Harpokrates had lame legs since he was fathered by a ghost, or the spirit of Osiris, and not by a real human being. His frailty may be also related to the difficult conditions at birth and the constant ordeals his mother had to endure to protect him from Set, his uncle and the murderer of his father. While he, symbolically, represents the fragility of a psychic content that is engendered under conflict, he also carries a transforming power. Horus, his adult form, takes revenge for the death of his father, and reassumes the place of the sovereign usurped by his uncle. Harpokrates symbolizes the rising sun and a new life, and can be understood from the psychic point of view as a function which conciliates life and death. He gives balance to the duality of the opposing ends. Harpokrates can also be seen as the result of the union between life (Isis) and death (Osiris).

Figure 6.4 Haprokrates on a lotus surrounded by Uroborus (drawing based on the Papyrus of Dama Heroub, 21st Dynasty, Egypt).

Harpokrates, with his thumb in his mouth, was adored by the Greeks as the god of silence, discretion, or secrecy. However, this same gesture might also allude to the fact that he is still only a child, referring to his dependence on his mother. On the other hand, Harpokrates represents a rare moment of creativity by rising from the chaotic depths and sitting on the lotus flower while being surrounded by the protection of the serpent. The protection of the mysterious powers is necessary for the great transforming process of Yesterday and Tomorrow, which requires an attitude of deep concentration and self-attention as implied by the act of sucking one's thumb. Because Harpokrates is also associated with healing practices in the Hellenic world, this gesture signals the need of concentration and introversion so that the regenerating and renovating powers can be united. In this image, we can see that a mystery is not to be revealed. Hence, the idea of silence.

When I began working on this subject, I searched for similar iconography in the Americas where a stomapod that is, an anthropomorphic image with the foot in the mouth, would be represented. So far, I have found only one similar image, on a large funerary vase coming from Marajó Island. A small anthropomorphic figure with the right foot on the mouth resides close to the rim (Figures 6.5 and 6.6).

Figures 6.5 and 6.6 A *camucin* (funerary urn) showing an anthropomorphic image with a foot on the mouth.

Here, the association between the stomapod and death and resurrection is more obvious, especially because this vase is a *camucim*, a Tupi-Guarani word meaning "funerary urn." It is more common to find images of anthropomorphic figures bringing one or both hands to the mouth. Such representations can be seen on several *camucins* and as adornment for ceremonial vases belonging to both the Marajó and Tapajó Indians. In contrast, the image of bringing the hands to the mouth may have a different connotation than bringing the foot to the mouth. For example, in the west wall at the Osireion at Abydos, there is an image of the corpse of the Sun God at the end of the sixth hour in which he is encircled by a seven-headed serpent while his hand is sustained against his mouth. This representation is the sign of the living power of the god and is, therefore, associated with his regenerative capacity.

Another divine entity, called Jurupari, comes to mind among the Tupi-Guarani speaking groups. The Jesuits, who for many decades were in charge of the catechization of the Brazilian Indians, utilized this supernatural being to personify the image of the Devil. This fact, however, is not so remarkable since these missionaries deemed that all systems of religious cult among the Indians were demonic. The graphic representation of Jurupari, however, bears some characteristics which are important for this discussion. It usually appeared at night and was responsible for bringing bad dreams. Etymologically, *Jurupari* means "mouth, hand, over; take out from the mouth."[17] Another variant of the name is *Jurupoary*, which has been translated as the "one who visits us in our hammock."[18] So, Jurupari is "the being who visits us at night, brings us nightmares and grabs our throat so impeding us to speak or shout."[19] Therefore, the icons with the hands on the mouth (sometimes on the cheek) could be connected to Jurupari, for he was feared and avoided since he was the one who brought bad dreams and breathlessness. And, as for any other ancient culture, bad dreams were an ominous happening that threatened one's daily life. From one perspective, if the hand on the mouth suggests the necessary introversion for the renewal of life (as in Harpokrates), then we can see how this same gesture in Jurupari's lore can also allude to terror.

There is another image belonging to the Gnostic theosophy where a nude child, stroking a skull, is surrounded by the Uroboric snake (Figure 6.7).

We can see the inscription *Pedet Finis Aborigine* ("Look for the end at the beginning") as an allusion to the necessity of understanding the universe in reverse time. It is as if we were visiting the Garden of Eden before the act of creation. This image can also be understood psychologically as the moment when the opposites are overcome and the return to unity is imminent. Everything that has been separated is now reunited. The child, as the prospective representation of the beginning of life, strokes the skull, indicating the end of this process. Symbolically, the skull, like all bones, can be understood as the part of the individual that does not perish. Bones resist death; thus, this image speaks to the everlasting that is born anew, or rather, the new birth of the everlasting.

Both the Tapajoara statuette and the adult Narayana figure are exclusively anthropomorphic Uroboric representations; therefore, they may point to a different

Figure 6.7 An anthropozoomorphic Uroborus (drawing based on Wither, G. (1635). *A Collection of Emblemes, Ancient and Modern*).

level of development. The Narayana figure alludes to a deep level of self-control in a male's psychology, so that a higher level of consciousness can be achieved. Here the individual is able to detach from his male instincts (erection and ejaculation) and is able to control and guide them towards illumination, that is, towards the Self. In this way, Narayana portrays an achievement of a higher level of consciousness.

It is not possible to assume that the Tapajoara statuette stands for a situation of control and detachment of instincts in a female's psychology akin to Narayana's representation of sexual self-control. Nonetheless, what has been discussed here does not preclude the hypothesis that the Tapajoara statuette may stand for something else that transcends the idea of human finite existence upon physical death. According to Eastern mythology, the big toe in the mouth is usually interpreted as *Infinity* when applied to time, and as *Eternity* when referred to the being.[20] This interpretation is meaningful because it presupposes the understanding of human existence on a much higher level. That is, whenever an individual psychologically experiences the objectivity of the Self, one also experiences the infinitude and the eternity of life.

It is important to point out that illumination is represented by an image in which the individual keeps oneself in a position of isolation and introspection. The iconography portrays the person encountering an image of God inside oneself. In other words, God is not a value found outside, but is emulated from the essence of the being. This, however, is a condition which is not new or strange in other traditions, such as Brahmanism or Gnosticism. In these creeds, the figures of Atman and Anthropos, respectively, stand for the microcosm inside a human being. Therefore, it is up to each individual to come to terms with the infinite and eternal divine portions that dwell within, so that he or she can reside in them. This requires a higher level of existential understanding, which presupposes a differentiated consciousness that is not fettered by collective values.

A similar condition can also be observed in the Christian tradition when Jesus tells a man who longs for eternal life to "go, sell everything you have and give to the poor, and you will have treasure in heaven" (Mark 10:21). From a symbolic point of view, this passage means that eternal life, life in God, or, psychologically speaking, life under the auspices of the Self, requires the abandonment of collective values and a deep dive into one's own essence and genuineness.

Therefore, the anthropomorphic Uroborus portrayed by both the Narayana figure and the Tapajoara statuette may evoke the return to Unity since they represent the individual's transformation process in which consciousness dwells in the Self.

From a practical point of view, it is not uncommon to see analysands who have sucked or still suck their thumbs, or have dreams where other segments of the body are brought to the mouth. The first thought such a behavior or oneiric material entices is that some sort of nourishment is lacking and is not obtainable from "normal" sources. It could also suggest that the individual is not getting the nutrition he or she needs.

For example, men have reported dreams where they appear to be sucking their own penises. Such images could be primarily understood as man's possibility or need to be fertilized by himself, or to get nutrition from what is more fertile and virile from himself. But by being so, what is the background behind the unconscious sending this kind of message? What is being compensated for individually or collectively? Maybe the answer can be found in the way we live today. Today's lifestyle is markedly extroverted and the collective demands for social and financial stability are high. The attributes that are required for so-called "personal success" are multiple and progressively demanding. They function like threats to human sanity. But no matter how much these requirements are fulfilled, our consulting offices are filled with patients who bear a perennial sense of lack of existential meaning. Therefore, images such as these, that is, sucking one's own penis, may indicate, in a metaphorical sense, the need or urgency to re-encounter the creative potential present in each one of us. The exercise of being creative is, indeed, the realization of the eternal in ourselves!

The theme of resurrection and immortality that is bound to the Uroborus may be further explored in the Egyptian Book of the Dead. In the book *Osireion at*

Abydos, Margaret A. Murray describes an image in the Book of the Dead where Osiris is depicted with his feet turned back until they touch the head. In this image, Osiris encircles the Duat (the Netherworld through which the resurrecting sun, Ra, is supposed to go), and from this position he supports Nut on his head (Figure 6.8). This Uroboric image of Osiris indicates that the sun, which dies every evening, is born anew of Nut every morning. The circular depiction of Osiris is rare, and occurs only on the sarcophagus of Seti I and in the tomb of Ramesses VI.[21] Here, though, Osiris's feet are not brought directly into the mouth, but to the back of the head.

A similar motif, also from Egyptian mythology, brings in the Earth-god Geb, the consort of Nut, the Sky-goddess. There are several depictions of these two gods, the latter hanging above, bent and touching the former, thus representing

Figure 6.8 Uroboric Osiris (drawing based on Plate XIII, Book of Gates, in Murray, M. A., Milne, J. G., & Crum, W. E. (1904). *The Osireion at Abydos*. London: B. Quaritch Collection, p. 12).

Figure 6.9 Geb's twisted-back posture (drawing based on the papyrus of the Book of the Dead of Henuttawy, the British Museum).

the cosmos. In one of these depictions, Geb appears in a twisted-back posture, which is connected to the acrobatic ritual dance of life and death. Usually, Geb is lying on his back, with both arms stretched out, but in this image, his lower limbs are brought up so that they touch the upper part of his face. This particular image, according to Jack Lindsay, "is especially linked with death, and the circular twist-back of the body must have something of the sense of completion, of merged ends and beginnings."[22] A variant of this depiction can be found in the Funerary Papyrus of the Chantress of Amun Henuttawy during the Third Intermediate Period (1070 BCE to 945 BCE), which depicts an image of Geb arching on his back, practicing autofellatio beneath Osiris in ithyphallic representation (Figure 6.9). This image brings together the regenerative, creative, and self-sustainable intentions, as well the sense of completeness, all present in the Uroboric form.

Upon analyzing these Uroboric representations from typically zoomorphic images to exclusive anthropomorphic ones, there is the idea that some sort of rebirth is implicit in them and, therefore, life is something perennial. The renewed birth points to the resurging of a new higher consciousness. The images of Osiris, Geb, and Nut, and perhaps the Tapajoara statuette, might each suggest that life is a continuum that must go through a process of constant death and rebirth.

Notes

1 Iyer, P. S. Khrishna (n.d.). *Tales from the Bhagavatham retold for Children*. http://vahini.org/downloads/sbtalesfc.html, p. 236 ff.
2 Wilhelm, R. (Trans.), & Baynes, C. F. (Trans.) (1968). *The I Ching or book of changes: the Richard Wilhelm translation*. London: Routledge & Kegan Paul.

3 Campbell, J. (1968). *The hero with a thousand faces*. Princeton, NJ: Princeton University Press, p. 41.
4 Editors of *Hinduism Today*. (2007). *What is Hinduism? Modern adventures into a profound global faith*. Kapaa: Himalayan Academy, p. 151.
5 Mindlin, B. (2003). *Moqueca de maridos: Mitos eróticos*. Lisboa: Caminho, p. 72.
6 Schaden, E. (1989). *A mitologia heróica de tribos indígenas do Brasil: Ensaio etnossociológico*. Rio de Janeiro: Ministero da educação e cultura, p. 145.
7 Knight, R. P. (1974). *A discourse on the worship of Priapus: and its connection with the mystic theology of the ancients*. Secaucus, NJ: University Books, p. 18.
8 Chevalier, J., Gheerbrant, A., & Buchanan-Brown, J. (2008). *The Penguin dictionary of symbols*. London: Penguin, p. 1012.
9 Schuchard, M. K. (2006). *Why Mrs Blake cried: William Blake and the sexual basis of spiritual vision*. London: Century, p. 73.
10 Ibid.
11 Moor, E. [1810] (2010). *The Hindu pantheon*. Whitefish, MT: Kessinger, p. 103.
12 Schuchard, M. K. (2006). *Why Mrs Blake cried: William Blake and the sexual basis of spiritual vision*. London: Century, p. 71.
13 Ibid.
14 Maclagan, E. R., & Russell, A. G. (Eds) (1904). *The prophetic books of William Blake: Jerusalem*. London: A. H. Bullen.
15 Ibid., p. xix.
16 Jung, C. G. (1979). *Symbols of transformation*, CW 5, § 146.
17 Magalhães, G. C., Magalhães, D. C., & Moreira, V. (1975). *O selvagem: Ed. comemorativa do centenário da 1ª ed*. Belo Horizonte: Ed. Itatiaia, p. 126 *n*.
18 Ibid.
19 Ibid.
20 Moor, E. [1810] (2010). *The Hindu pantheon*. Whitefish, MT: Kessinger, p. 105.
21 Murray, M. A., Milne, J. G., & Crum, W. E. (1904). *The Osireion at Abydos*. London: B. Quaritch Collection, p. 12.
22 Lindsay, J. (1970). *The origins of alchemy in Graeco-Roman Egypt*. London: Muller, p. 274 ff.

Chapter 7

Final considerations

Analytical psychology is always leading us towards the understanding of the archetypal dispositions that are organized and act in the background of our existential drama. Many of our symptoms, difficulties, and sufferings, and even the stagnation of psychic life, conceal values which, if their meanings are accessed, reveal themselves as gates to be opened to the person. Getting through this portal allows one to reach his or her condition of being an individual. While the ego, if healthy, maintains the function of discriminating and manages the whole process, the great mover of all this unfolding is grounded in the archetypes of the unconscious, which contain the dynamos of such an enterprise. However, to unveil these aprioristic psychic representations brings forth a challenge because their language is symbolic. In other words, that which belongs to the unconscious and causes a primary impression on the ego is the "best expression of something inexpressible,"[1] that is, a symbol.

Moreover, because the language of the unconscious is symbolic, the best method or approach that brings us closer to a symbol's meaning is to visit and investigate the varied available structures that guard any kind of analogy to the image under investigation. This speaks, then, to the character of mystery that permeates the archetype and the transpersonal value that is contained in the unconscious. To visit such a domain, the ego must have a great capacity to accommodate the various and multifaceted dispositions that are concealed in the image. This is, indeed, the approach of this book—an insistent visitation to the various possibilities of understanding. It is probable that the only possible way to fully realize our humanity is through the knowledge and integration of the archetypal images that occur to us, accompanied by a given relativization of the convictions and pragmatism that are usually kindred to the structure of the ego.

In spite of the individual dreams that motivated this study, the material we investigated has, above all, a transpersonal character. We can recognize that we are facing an archetypal image when its emotional charge invades us to the point that we feel shaken in our convictions or in the customary anchors we use every day. The childhood dream that was mentioned in the Introduction of this book, for instance, bears such a characteristic. Its numinous nature could be testified not only by the elements presented in the dream image (cavern, jewels, wonderful feet, divine being, pool of naturally warm water) but, above all, by its effect, which continued to reverberate in the analysand's psychology in the subsequent decades of his life.

The intention in writing this book was to explore the possible symbolic parallelism between the phylogenetic development of the lower limbs and the ontogeny of consciousness. Generally speaking, it was an attempt to understand some aspects of consciousness in connection to the elements that accompanied human development. Investigations such as this, therefore, offer a basic presupposition that should permeate each and every individual's experience, since the search for meaning is at the heart of the human condition. Analytical psychology primarily takes a teleological standpoint and constantly invites us to ask ourselves "What is the meaning?" or "Where will this lead us?" in respect to a given issue. Therefore, it was necessary to extensively investigate the motifs of the feet and the lower limbs so that several ways of approaching these themes could emerge with their multiple psychological understandings. What then, would the intention of the unconscious be if it emphasizes so vividly, both psychically and physically, these precise body segments in someone's life, as illustrated by the analysands' experiences?

The parallel suggested here between the neurodevelopment of the lower limbs and the process of consciousness acquisition may not be unreasonable, since, one can say, these bodily segments have in themselves a teleology in their functioning. Locomotion is, surely, a possible means to acquire and expand consciousness. Even in its physical objective aspect, through body displacement, an individual can redimension himself or herself upon meeting the "other" by venturing to other lands, discovering new cultures, and meeting distinct peoples. In its subjective aspect, a human being only transforms and develops when the psychic processes display a certain amount of "mobility," which allows the individual to transit between the polarities of existence and the conflict of the opposites. Only then may the person find, internally, an adequate accommodation for the highest value within, that is, the Self. The "transit" is a mandatory condition in the toil between conscious and unconscious. One day we might get close to an understanding; another day we might stumble on a rather obscure unconscious domain. Then we return back to the light of consciousness, but once more we penetrate the hidden places of our personality. This process goes on *ad aeternum*. Not to move, subjectively or objectively, is a *quasi mortis imago*.

There is still no final answer to the symbolic parallelism I have proposed, in spite of the amount of material that was gathered, because the possible answers are varied and multifaceted. If, however, we could point to one factor that permeates all the analogous and correlated images discussed in this book, it would be the question of creativity. Consciousness and creativity, therefore, constitute a binomium that should not be conceived separately. The lower limbs, especially the feet, are bodily structures whose symbology is deeply linked to the creative process.

When the Tapajoara statuette "intruded" into the discussions in the analytical setting, it was as if a new bud began to sprout out of this stem of investigation.

This important icon prompted me to deeply research the Brazilian culture, whose richness still remains to be uncovered. Consequently, it also fostered multiple inquiries into our Brazilian psyche: Why did these people model an image as such? What were their motivations? What kind of conscious apparatus did these Indians have? Following the words of Demokritos as mentioned earlier, the Tapajoara statuette did cause an impression; she impregnated us with herself! Once we committed ourselves to her, a vast road was unveiled, ready to be further investigated no matter how obscure she still is. This image of a female bringing her big toe to her mouth added a great amount of libido to the issue of creativity, which was already growing out of the symbolism of the lower limbs that I had been researching.

There are some other ways to look at the childhood dream at the beginning of this book. Maybe it would suffice to say that, in spite of being four to five years old at the time, this man's unconscious had already posed the question of creativity to him in a rather remarkable way, considering the numinous impression and everlasting effect it caused on him. It seems that the synchronistic aspect of the insurgence of this statuette in our discussions wanted to emphasize, therefore, that creativity is the one aspect which demands constant nourishing. But it is a kind of nurturing that should be carried on by means of what the individual may discover within, or eventually be able to put forth in the outer world.

The way the dream affected the patient made the archetypal qualities of the experience quite evident, especially because of the fear and even the terror that had accompanied him throughout his life. Situations like this usually paralyze us, for it is as if we are facing something so powerful that it can destroy us. It is not without reason that many personifications of unconscious numinous content in art bring us images of monsters to be combated and defeated. The required need for transformation in order to overcome the vicissitudes of daily life in search for meaning requires a constant creative disposition. And this is dreadful because there are numerous monsters to fight off within our deepest subjectivity. The much-praised "fear of God" in Christianity, then, could be understood psychologically in this way: What wants to be realized in us is always appalling to the ego. It is horrifying and distressing because it is an archetypal disposition which, in other words, belongs to the domain of the gods.

Obviously, there are many other aspects of this subject matter that need to be further explored and investigated. The material presented in this book, even though it may appear excessive at times, is still very modest considering the scope. I was told that von Franz often pointed out that whenever we are facing an image from which there is not precise information or a solid basis upon which we can build a robust hypothesis concerning its meaning, we should collect as much correlated material as possible in order to pave a road towards symbolical understanding. Therefore, the amount of material gathered for this book and the analysis of it are pertinent for that matter. Metaphorically, we can think about how the Nile River needs to go through a process of overflowing, or inflating itself, so that after it recedes, its banks become ready to be fertilized. In this way, it is my hope that, after visiting the many myths and legends presented in this book, each individual reader will germinate his or her own views on the subject.

In any event, it appears that the unconscious itself indicated to me that the overflow had reached an adequate level. As I was working on this last chapter, I had the following dream:

> I dreamed I was pregnant and about to deliver. I went to a "hospital" and the nurse "examined" me and confirmed that it was my due time. So, I stayed there and the contractions began.

Much different from lay expectations, the analytical process does not always "resolve" an issue posed by an analysand, neither ending nor bringing a solution to its demands. Instead, such a process is more akin to the word "cure," taken from the Greek *Komei* (κομέω), meaning "to take care" or "to attend." This signifies that the psychic cure may be more related to the act of creating consciousness or understanding that which is obscure. Certainly, what indeed mitigates psychic suffering is understanding.

When the alchemists utilized the expression "divine water," they were talking about the substance of the Self, emphasizing its double character that bears not only the creative power of life, but also death.[2] It signifies that the extraction of meaning, or the creation of consciousness, has the power to "save" us, while remaining unconscious implies perishment. Our human destiny is, therefore, inexorably connected to the need to move beyond the paralyzing forces of the opposites that we face in life. And in a creative way!

Notes

1 Jung C. G. (1977). *Psychological Types*, CW 6, § 815.
2 Jung C. G. (1970). *Mysterium Coniunctionis*, CW 14, § 105.

Index